APPLYING LEAN IN HEALTHCARE

A Collection of International Case Studies

Edited by Joe Aherne • John Whelton

Foreword by Jeffrey Clothier, MD

The Leading Edge Group

CRC Press
Taylor & Francis Group
Boca Raton London New York

CRC Press is an imprint of the
Taylor & Francis Group, an **informa** business

A PRODUCTIVITY PRESS BOOK

Productivity Press
Taylor & Francis Group
270 Madison Avenue
New York, NY 10016

© 2010 by Leading Edge Ireland Limited
Productivity Press is an imprint of Taylor & Francis Group, an Informa business

No claim to original U.S. Government works

Printed in the United States of America on acid-free paper
10 9 8 7 6 5 4 3 2 1

International Standard Book Number: 978-1-4398-2739-0 (Hardback)

Library of Congress Cataloging-in-Publication Data

Applying lean in healthcare : a collection of international case studies / edited by Joe
    Aherne and John Whelton.
        p. ; cm.
    Includes bibliographical references and index.
    ISBN 978-1-4398-2739-0 (alk. paper)
    1. Health services administration. I. Aherne, Joe. II. Whelton, John.
    [DNLM: 1. Delivery of Health Care--organization & administration. 2. Delivery
of Health Care--economics. 3. Efficiency, Organizational. 4. Organizational Case
Studies. 5. Quality Assurance, Health Care--methods. W 84.1 A6527 2010]

    RA971.A815 2010
    362.1068--dc22

2009043908

Visit the Taylor & Francis Web site at
http://www.taylorandfrancis.com

and the Productivity Press Web site at
http://www.productivitypress.com

Contents

Foreword

As healthcare costs increase at a faster rate than the cost of other products or services, healthcare providers—in particular, hospitals—are under continuous pressure to dramatically improve service and patient safety, and to reduce costs, waiting times, and errors and associated litigation. However, hospitals are not making the necessary improvements in cost, quality, and safety. A report by the U.S. Health and Human Services Office of the Inspector General finds that 20 percent of consecutive inpatient stay sequences were associated with poor quality care, unnecessary fragmentation of care, or both. The current organization and management of hospitals form an imperfect system that cannot effectively address these issues. Major projects to restructure hospitals, dramatically reduce costs, and improve customer care have had little impact on quality or cost.

In simplistic terms, current healthcare systems are not designed to make the process or "value stream" of care flow smoothly. Healthcare services are often "batch and queue," with patients spending most of their time waiting until the healthcare professional is ready—that is, push versus pull. As the population matures, patient cycle times in the hospitals, post-care facilities, and laboratories become key measurements that need to improve.

My belief is that Lean Healthcare can provide a solution to address some of these concerns successfully with minimal cost but maximum benefit. *Applying Lean in Healthcare—A Collection of International Case Studies* gives us a snapshot of what can be done through adopting a structured approach to Lean in healthcare.

Hospitals are made up of a series of processes with diverse lines of business. Consequently, they need to build their delivery systems with these lines of business in mind. Hospitals need to know the businesses that drive 80 percent of their value proposition. They need to streamline their organization systems and processes to support fully the process required to deliver high-quality care. Commitment and support for any Lean initiative need to come not only from top healthcare management but, even more critically, from the "bottom up" for implementation. Decision making and system development need to be pushed to the lowest levels of any healthcare organization. Each chapter of *Applying Lean in Healthcare* is full of examples of how groups of healthcare professionals have educated themselves on Lean principles and worked together on projects to achieve improvements in efficiencies across a diverse range of processes, such as laboratory supplies, an outpatient antenatal clinic, and a medical oncology unit.

Management consultants are normally engaged as Lean change agents rather than as Lean facilitators. Healthcare staff should lead any Lean implementation program. These people are best equipped to understand the work environment, issues, challenges, and what will work and what won't. An empowered and knowledgeable team is therefore essential to achieve sustainable improvements and long-term success in any Lean initiative. Put simply, Lean will not work without an educated workforce. The successful projects emanating from The Leading Edge Group Lean Healthcare Green Belt and Black Belt programs fully validate this assertion.

With this in mind, I am privileged to have been asked to write the foreword for this publication. I have worked closely with The Leading Edge Group for a number of years and I am always amazed by the enthusiasm and zeal that both Joe Aherne and John Whelton show in promoting Lean in healthcare. Their Lean Healthcare Green Belt and Black Belt programs have been enthusiastically received throughout the healthcare world and many of these associated projects are included in the following chapters.

I hope healthcare professionals can learn from the different approaches adopted in this publication and that it will act as a catalyst for future positive change in all our healthcare systems.

Dr. Jeffrey Clothier, MD
Medical Director of the UAMS Psychiatric Research Institute
Associate Professor, University of Arkansas for Medical Sciences,
Department of Psychiatry

Acknowledgments

This book is dedicated to all the thousands of healthcare professionals and individuals who have steadfastly supported improvement initiatives within their own organizations. These initiatives have invariably produced significant cost and process efficiencies, with the primary focus of improving the overall quality of patient care. In this book, we highlight only a fraction of what has been achieved. We salute all those who actively foster and promote the benefits of Lean Healthcare.

We specifically thank those healthcare professionals and organizations who have contributed individual real-life case studies for the publication. We thank them for their permission to publish in detail the Lean approaches applied and lessons learned, for the benefit of all our readers.

Finally, we thank all those working for The Leading Edge Group for their unstinting loyalty and support in making this project a reality.

1

Introduction to Lean Healthcare

WHAT IS LEAN THINKING?

Lean Thinking has been defined as "the dynamic, knowledge-driven, and customer-focused process through which people in a defined enterprise continuously eliminate waste with the goal of creating value."[1]

Lean is regarded as a systematic approach to identifying and eliminating waste or non-value-added activities in a process through continuous improvement. The key focus of Lean Thinking is identifying the value of any given process by distinguishing value-added steps from non-value-added steps, and eliminating waste so that eventually every step adds value to that process. This is achieved by enabling the flow of a product or service at the pull of the customer in pursuit of perfection.

The origins of Lean Thinking go back more than forty years:

- Lean Thinking started in the 1960s in Japan with the development of the Toyota Production System (TPS). It was quickly established as a method for highly effective production of cars and related engineered components.
- The concept of Lean Thinking was introduced to the West in 1991 by the book *The Machine That Changed the World*,[2] written by Womack, Jones, and Roos. The book explores the differences between companies with traditional mass manufacturing systems and the TPS.
- A sequel to *The Machine That Changed the World*, called *Lean Thinking*,[3] was published in 1996. This became an international bestseller and extended the popularity and impact of Lean Thinking.

1

- Lean Thinking is now well established in the sophisticated world of aerospace and aircraft manufacture. Many other industries can also benefit from this approach. For example, the concept of Lean Thinking has now spread to pharmaceutical, medical, electronics, healthcare, and a host of related industries.

Lean Thinking is a philosophy that can be applied to a variety of organizations. This is because it focuses on processes. All organizations are made up of a series of processes, or sets of activities or steps intended to create value for those who are dependent on them—customers or patients. The principles associated with Lean Thinking include understanding customer value, introducing flow approaches, and the quest for perfection. All these can be applied to nonmanufacturing processes.

Continuing global expansion has made business in all industries more and more competitive. Using Lean Thinking to reduce and eliminate waste enables organizations to become more competitive because it enables them to:

- Operate more quickly and efficiently at lower costs
- Become more responsive to the needs of customers or patients
- Increase revenue levels
- Increase service levels

This can help organizations reach a world-class standard where employees experience increased job satisfaction and fulfillment, and customers receive the highest quality of service.

Lean Thinking is based on the application of a number of tools and strategies aimed at streamlining all aspects of a business process. These tools are intended to reduce the labor, space, capital, materials, equipment, and time involved in the delivery of the appropriate products or services to end customers.

LEAN AND HEALTHCARE

Lean Thinking is now being successfully applied to the healthcare industry. The philosophy is *not* intended to eliminate or reduce the number of employees working in the industry. It seeks only to eliminate waste in all tasks and processes so that time, materials, resources, and procedures can be utilized as efficiently as possible. This enables healthcare organizations to dedicate more time and effort to patient care without extra cost to the patient or organization. In summary, Lean Thinking can be used to:

- Decrease costs while increasing patient satisfaction
- Provide better quality healthcare while utilizing the same employees
- Increase healthcare employees' motivation and job satisfaction
- Improve and maintain a high quality of service

Although Lean is not the solution for every problem faced today in healthcare, it can certainly make some dramatic improvements that provide sustainable, positive improvements in a variety of areas, including:[4]

- Laboratory services
- Operating room procedures
- Accident and emergency (A&E) departments
- Healthcare employees
- Healthcare administration

Laboratory Services

Applying Lean Thinking can help increase the space required to carry out laboratory testing and sample analysis. This in turn helps to increase productivity, efficiency, and the accuracy of results, while decreasing the amount of time that patients have to wait to receive test results.

Operating Room Procedures

Applying Lean Thinking to operating room procedures can help reduce the time taken between operations, therefore increasing the number of procedures that can be undertaken in a day. Lean Thinking can also be used to increase operating room space and reduce the number of tools and amount of inventory used. This can help decrease the costs and make the operating room an easier and more effective location for surgeons and operating staff.

Accident and Emergency Departments

Lean Thinking can help reduce the amount of time that an A&E patient has to wait before receiving attention.

Healthcare Employees

By increasing patient satisfaction, improving the work environment, and potentially decreasing the long hours that healthcare employees have to endure, Lean Thinking can help improve job satisfaction, morale, and motivation, and make the industry a more attractive prospect for new staff.

Healthcare Administration

Lean Thinking can be used to improve the efficiency, speed, and costs involved in the administration and processing of patient information and any data used in the day-to-day running of a healthcare organization. Again, this helps these organizations to run more smoothly, and it increases patient satisfaction with the service that they are receiving.

Lean Thinking means that processes must be designed to ensure optimal results. Two of the main principles associated with the system are that all value is the result of a process, and that the appropriate process will produce the appropriate results. These principles are dependent on the skill, ability, performance, motivation, and commitment of the people involved in each process and the organization itself.

PRINCIPLES OF LEAN HEALTHCARE

The following principles are fundamental to Lean Thinking:[5]

- Specify value from the standpoint of the end customer.
- Identify the value stream for each product or service family.
- Eliminate waste.
- Make the product or service flow.
- Respond to the customer pull.
- Improve continuously in pursuit of perfection.
- Encourage employee contribution.

Specify Value from the Standpoint of the End Customer

Value provides a crucial starting point for the implementation of Lean within organizations. Value essentially consists of all activities that customers perceive as directly contributing to the creation, transformation, or delivery of the product or service that they have paid for.

In healthcare, value can be anything that improves the physical or mental state of the patient. Patients typically value prompt care treatment and fair and orderly processes (they don't mind waiting if it is for a good cause). They also value knowing a plan (they will put up with a lot if there is a plan), and staff who know the plan and appear to be working toward achieving it. However, an organization needs the flexibility to accommodate changes in its view of value, because this will evolve. For example, in healthcare we focus on any activity that has strong evidence that it helps patients get better and/or manages their symptoms and comfort. This means that as our knowledge (or the evidence) changes, our definition of "value" can also change.

The intention of any Lean initiative should be to get staff and managers to see what patients see as the parts of their journey through healthcare. You will achieve optimum results if you understand patients' viewpoints and include patients in any Lean initiative.[6]

Identify the Value Stream for Each Product or Service Family

The value stream is the end-to-end collection of processes that create and deliver value for the customer or patient. A value stream crosses departmental boundaries and typically incorporates only those steps or activities that add value as defined by the customer or patient.

The value stream can include people, tools, equipment, and technologies, as well as physical facilities, communication channels, and policies and procedures.

In industry, the value stream can be all the steps currently required to move a product or group of similar products from concept to launch, order to delivery, and delivery through recycling. In healthcare, the value stream can be the sequence of events that make up the patient journey.

In identifying the value stream, it is important to challenge every step, asking why each activity is necessary.

Eliminate Waste

Anything that does not add value in the eyes of the patient is viewed as wasteful; it is a non-value-added activity. Waste is typically the result of how a system or process is structured or organized.

Activities or elements in any process should therefore be classified as:

- Value-added
- Non-value-added but necessary
- Non-value-added—waste

Value-Added

Value-adding activities make a product or service more valuable from the customer's perspective. To be value added, the action must meet all three of the following criteria:

- The customer must be able to see how the activity adds value to a product or enhances the service provided.
- The action or activity must be carried out correctly in the first instance.
- The action must somehow change the product or service in a particular way.

An example of such an activity in healthcare would be the diagnosis and treatment of an illness or injury.

Non-Value-Added but Necessary

These activities do not add value to a product or service from the customer's perspective, but are necessary unless the existing process is modified. An example of such an activity in healthcare would be an update to patient documentation that does not directly affect the level of care a patient will receive, but is necessary for a complete patient file. For example, if you update details such as a mailing address for a patient who is in the hospital for a surgical procedure, this will usually not affect the type or level of care that patient will receive. However, it is necessary for future correspondence.

Non-Value-Added—Waste

These activities do not add value to a product or service from the patient's perspective, and they are not necessary in the existing process. Patients need to have a clear perception that value is being added. They need to feel that they are getting value for what they are actually paying for. Organizations need to adopt a customer perspective when assessing exactly what value is. For example, poor room design or inappropriate placement of equipment might make it unnecessarily difficult for staff to administer care to patients.

Waste can be defined as any element of a process that adds time, effort, or cost but no value. Waste within any process is costly, and it directly affects profitability and resources. It means staff time is used inefficiently. This can have a negative effect on staff motivation if they perceive such work as ineffective. Activity mapping will help you to uncover where this waste is occurring. Waste may manifest itself through inefficient planning or scheduling processes or any non-value-adding activities.

Taiichi Ohno, the founding father of the TPS, compiled seven types of waste. Table 1.1 outlines examples of these types of waste in the healthcare sector.

TABLE 1.1

Types of Waste in Healthcare

Types of Waste	Explanation/Example
1. Overproduction	Blood draws done early before the decision to complete blood tests has been made
2. Transportation	Extra travel required for blood samples
3. Inventory (work in progress)	Test results awaiting distribution; excess documentation, patient forms, and supplies
4. Processing	Excessive documentation; excessive health insurance processing
5. Waiting	Patients sitting in a waiting room waiting for an appointment or consultation; patients in A&E units waiting to be seen by a doctor or nurse
6. Correction/making defective products	Medication prescription errors; incorrect patient information for diagnosis/treatment
7. Motion	Looking for missing patient information; sharing medical equipment/tools

Since the conception of the TPS, new types of waste have been categorized.[7] These are specific to all business processes:

- Untapped human potential
- Waste of inappropriate systems
- Wasted energy and water
- Wasted materials
- Service and office waste
- Waste of customer or patient time
- Defecting customers or patients

Something should not be branded as waste unless the total value stream has been assessed. In a Lean enterprise, taking time out that does not add value is far more important than speeding up individual work processes or activities. The emphasis must be on eliminating waste with the goal of creating value that can apply to all stakeholders. (A stakeholder is an individual or group with an interest in maintaining the success of an organization and upholding the viability of the organization's products and services.)

You must manage and eliminate the seven wastes in order to streamline a system and run wards more efficiently. Once you have succeeded in eliminating the waste, your next step should be waste prevention. Ensure you design new services without inherently wasteful steps.

Make the Product or Service Flow[8]

Once value has been clearly defined, the value stream identified, and obvious wasteful steps removed, the next step is to make the value-creating steps flow. All the steps that truly create value should be analyzed and ordered so that they occur in rapid sequence. The principle should be based on the idea that, in general, things flow better when done in order of arrival, not in batches. To reduce unnecessary waits, you need to reduce piles of paperwork and units of work and reduce batching or batch sizes in areas such as diagnostic testing and patient waiting areas.

Ideally, every step in the process should be right every time and always available. It should be flexible to meet changing customer demand and optimized to avoid bottlenecks, without being oversized.

All areas should be in constant open communication regarding schedules, relevant information, available materials, equipment, and resources. This is easier to achieve once waste is eliminated and value is identified. Processes should be organized to meet specific customer or patient needs based on minimum inventory levels and bottlenecks within the process.

In a healthcare organization such as a hospital, the goal should be to achieve continuous smooth flow throughout all hospital processes so that patients receive the maximum level of care on time, and of the highest quality. It is important to implement flow by starting at the end of the patient journey and the diagnostic pathway and working backwards. This is because, as all the waiting lists and piles of work are done, they move onto the next stage in the process.

Respond to the Customer Pull

Pull refers to the actual customer demand that drives a business process. It is a system based on a cascading process from downstream to upstream activities in which nothing is produced by the upstream supplier until the downstream customer signals a need.

Processes should be organized to meet specific customer or patient needs based on minimum inventory levels and bottlenecks within the process. This is based on a pull system where materials, equipment, documentation, and resources are pulled through the system based on customer or patient requirements, rather than a push system where materials are pushed through the system to suit operational needs or simply because capacity requirements are available.

An example of pull in healthcare is when tests on samples are scheduled and carried out based on when the patient requires them rather than batching and storing the samples because of machine efficiency needs.

Improve Continuously in Pursuit of Perfection

Perfection refers to any ongoing activity that is aimed at achieving better results. Perfection is an ideal, so anything and everything can be improved. Following are some principles in seeking perfection:

- Maintaining that the status quo is unacceptable
- Putting aside preconceived ideas

- Finding root causes to problems
- Focusing on the process, not the people
- Accepting that the employees are the experts
- Allowing yourself the right to fail

Lean Thinking is not about developing elaborate and expensive solutions that may take months and years to develop and implement. Rather, it reflects the commitment within a Lean organization to look for improvement opportunities on an ongoing basis.

Once improvements have been established, the Lean initiative should not finish there. Plans and strategies should be approved and put in place to ensure that improvements and efficiencies are sustained and become the norm rather than the exception. Any Lean initiative should reflect long-term as well as short-term improvement. Lean practices and strategies should be implemented with this in mind.

Once improvements have been implemented, information-gathering techniques such as surveys, scorecards, quality and performance metrics should be used to monitor and assess quality and cost levels and ensure that they are maintained consistently. The data gathered here can then be used to harness further improvements.

Encourage Employee Contribution

Successful Lean initiatives need high-performing, flexible, motivated, and multifunctional staff. Healthcare administrators need to gain commitment and trust from all employees for the Lean initiative to ensure its success.

Given that Lean is often focused on reducing costs by eliminating waste, there is a common misconception that the elimination of waste and cutting of costs involve reducing the workforce through layoffs. Such a belief can lead to employee fear, skepticism, and mistrust. It is vital that these fears are allayed immediately at the start of the Lean journey.

Having committed to a Lean initiative, healthcare administrators must make it clear to all employees that such an initiative will not involve any reduction in the workforce:

- Make it clear that the Lean initiative is aimed at utilizing existing materials, resources, and procedures as efficiently as possible.
- Outline that the benefits will not only extend to patients, but also to the work environment, making job roles and responsibilities more efficient and satisfying.
- Explain that it is an approach that helps empower employees to plan how and when to implement improvements to best meet patient requirements and expectations.

When implementing Lean, employees should be regarded as the most important element of the initiative. Healthcare management and administration should immediately seek employee involvement. Their ideas, suggestions, thoughts, and opinions should be taken into account when developing and implementing any Lean strategy.

By showing respect for employee opinions and contributions, healthcare organizations can gain full commitment to the Lean initiative. Any management strategy should be developed so as to help develop and maintain dedicated and high-performing employees. Where employee roles or responsibilities need to change, then existing employees should be retrained if necessary, rather than any new employees recruited. These people have invaluable experience in existing processes and procedures, so their continuing contribution and involvement throughout the Lean implementation is vital. Employee needs, as well as patient needs, should be catered to in any implementation of Lean.

REFERENCES

1. Murman, E. M. et al. 2002. *Lean enterprise value: Insights from MIT's Lean Aerospace Initiative.* New York: Palgrave: New York.
2. Womack, J. P., D. T. Jones, and D. Roos. 1990. *The machine that changed the world.* New York: Rawson Associates.
3. Womack, J. P., and D. T. Jones, D. T. 1996. *Lean Thinking.* London: Simon & Schuster.
4. http://www.projmasters.com/LeanHealthCare.htm.
5. http://www.lean.org/WhatsLean/Principles.cfm.

6. http://www.institute.nhs.uk/quality_and_service_improvement_tools/quality_and_service_improvement_tools/lean.html.
7. Bicheno, J. 2000. *The Lean toolbox,* 2nd ed. Buckingham, U.K.: Picsie Books.
8. http://www.nodelaysscotland.scot.nhs.uk/ServiceImprovement/Tools/Pages/IT227_FlowReduceUnnecessaryWaits.aspx.

FURTHER READING

The Lean office: Collected practices and cases. New York: Productivity Press, 2005.
Chalice, Robert W. *Stop rising healthcare costs using Toyota Lean Production Methods: 38 steps for improvement.* Milwaukee, WI: ASQ Quality Press Publications, 2005.

2

Making It Lean

Hilary Grey
Aptium Cancer Care, Knutsford, Cheshire, U.K.

PROJECT BACKGROUND

Aptium Cancer Care

Aptium Cancer Care, a subsidiary of U.S.-based Aptium Oncology, was established in the United Kingdom in 2006. The company objective is to bring the clinical and business knowledge gained from more than twenty years' experience providing cancer care in the United States to help improve patients' cancer care experience in the United Kingdom.

Our model is patient focused. Ours is an outpatient-based service that includes chemotherapy, radiotherapy, and all the supportive care needed to support individuals undergoing cancer treatment.

The Aptium U.K. and U.S. operations use Lean methodology to increase efficiency and to provide the highest level of patient care at a competitive price. In our view, the waste arising from non-Lean practices is simply too expensive. This waste also draws valuable resources away from the only thing that really matters—caring for patients.

Why Lean?

An important principle of Lean is the constant pursuit of perfection. Lean is a journey, rather than a goal. No matter how Lean we might be at the beginning, non-Lean practices easily creep in, and our model recognizes the need to constantly examine and improve the way we do things. Aptium Oncology in the United States has already incorporated

Lean methodology into some of its existing facilities, but Aptium Cancer Care in the United Kingdom is in a different position. Rather than having to change existing ways of working to *make them Lean*, we are allowing Lean to inform every aspect of our business and clinical models, *right from the start*.

The Aptium model is designed to deliver excellent patient care and employee satisfaction cost-effectively. It does this by promoting the use of Lean principles. Lean aims to add value and eliminate waste. The following definition of Lean Thinking is posted in our offices:

> We use dynamic, knowledge-driven, and customer-focused processes through which people in a defined enterprise continuously eliminate waste with the goal of creating value.

As we present our model in a variety of settings, we demonstrate how a patient's desire to live his or her life fully becomes a catalyst for Lean activities. We understand the patient does not want to be at the center but instead wants to be at home, or work, or play.

Why Is Lean Important in Healthcare?

Cost and cost containment in healthcare is an increasingly sensitive issue in the United Kingdom. The clinical governance framework and regulatory agencies (such as the Nursing and Midwifery Council) require that evidence-based practice be in place, practice that is specific and patient focused. For example, people want short waiting times for the highest quality care, delivered by expert and professional staff—in other words, people want the "value" that is the cornerstone of Lean thinking.

It is widely recognized that waste is a problem within the healthcare industry. This is not just about money or supplies, but also about time and effort, which have an associated cost. For example, the patient who arrives late for an appointment because of poor parking facilities could potentially delay doctors and nurses. The waste of time and energy searching for missing records can delay patients and consultants. This has a ripple effect. Lean aims to reduce or eliminate waste of all types continuously, which results in decreased costs and increased satisfaction for both patients and staff.

IMPLEMENTING LEAN

Rolling Out and Sustaining a Clinical Business Model

Implementing the Aptium model in the United Kingdom followed the process outlined below, drawing on the experience gained in the United States and, where appropriate, adapting the tools used there to fit the new environment.

The process involved the following steps:

1. Develop a culture rather than a concept:
   a. Hire the right people to ensure we have the right mind-set
   b. Train staff
   c. Involve staff
2. Develop end-to-end processes with all involved in that process:
   a. Use the "Ohno circle" (named after Taiichi Ohno, the Toyota engineer involved with developing Lean methodology) to review the implemented process constantly
   b. Use dashboards to report on a new process or Kaizen event
   c. Use our "safety rounds" to ensure the 5S improvements are continuous
   d. In our culture of no blame, use Kaizen and root-cause analysis to understand unexpected events in order to prevent them in the future
3. Continually review the process, using:
   a. Continuous education
   b. Continuous motivation
   c. Continuous evaluation

Developing a Culture

Lean is all about people, meeting the needs of the customer, and enabling employees to do the best possible job with the highest level of satisfaction. Therefore, it is essential to place the right people into the right posts. Part of the Aptium model for achieving Lean is appointing people with the right mind-set. We select people who have an open-minded approach, are keen to develop, and are not afraid of change. Recruitment advertisements and job descriptions are worded to attract dynamic, forward-thinking individuals to jobs at every level. Interviewers pose questions to identify the candidates who will be both able and willing to generate and perpetuate a Lean culture.

The induction process then provides an excellent opportunity to train new recruits in Lean principles and methods. Staff members are given specific training in Lean Thinking. They are given the clear message that Lean is not the latest management fad but a core value of the organization, as fundamental as professional integrity or good hygiene. Without Lean, it would simply not be possible for Aptium to achieve the required high level of patient care at a viable cost.

Once the right people are appointed, Lean principles and objectives are woven into their work life with Aptium. The job description is Lean-focused, and ongoing performance reviews deal with this element of the job.

Employees are required to show how they incorporate continuous incremental improvement into their daily work. This is an objective against which staff members are annually evaluated. All staff members are involved in Lean events, and staff meetings report on the results of Lean initiatives. We post dashboards (Figure 2.1) in the areas where the work is performed.

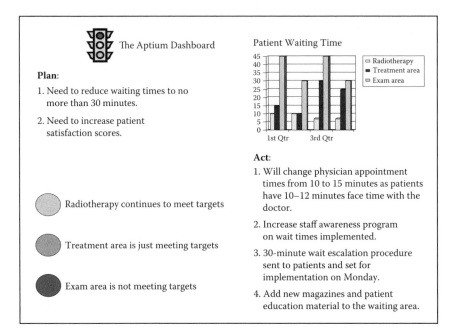

FIGURE 2.1

An Aptium dashboard showing wait time targets.

Occasionally, staff may be unwilling to enter into the Lean culture. In such cases, we try to bring about a series of quick but significant "wins" to show reluctant staff the benefits of Lean. Ongoing resistance is addressed by inviting the reluctant staff to communicate their reservations and also their ideas about how things should be done. We believe most people go to work with the intention of doing a good job. Because the evidence for Lean is clear, we are confident that the reluctant people will be won over to a Lean approach. This is essential because if staff members undermine the approach, it has a negative impact on others and the Lean initiative as a whole. Staff who are unable to incorporate Lean principles into their working practices must undertake a work improvement program as part of a disciplinary process.

Developing the End-to-End Process

Lean is all about mapping the end-to-end process. We learned in our Y2K IT implementation that mapping the process is a good opportunity to get to know the business. Representatives of all the teams need to be involved in the procedure. Involving the whole team adds understanding; a clinical person looks at a process in a way different from that of a finance person. For example, participating in clinical trials could benefit a patient. A doctor may simply see giving the drug as an opportunity to give the patient a chance to extend his or her life, a nurse may worry about how to deliver the drug, an administrator may have concerns about impact on staffing, while the finance person is keeping an eye on hidden costs. Each person comes to the table with his or her own agenda.

The process involves three basic steps:

1. Establish the goal of the process. This needs to reflect what the patients want and what the staff want:
   a. Patients want to get their treatment and leave.
   b. Staff want to provide safe and effective care.
2. Work out how the patient moves through the system at a high level, with a drilldown to specifics to see whether the process meets the goal (Figure 2.2).
   a. The constraints in the system are examined. This involves as many people as possible to discuss the effects of change on upstream or downstream procedures. For example, the laundry

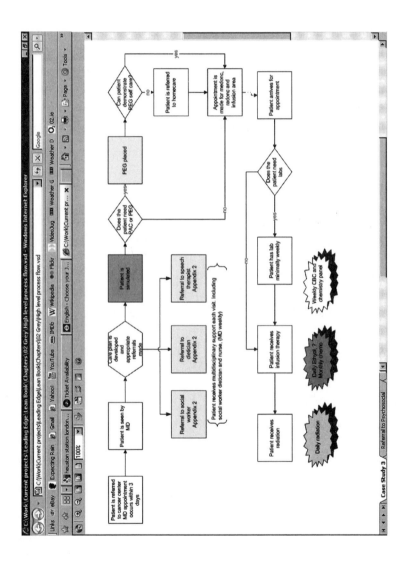

FIGURE 2.2

High-level process map showing the patient process for head and neck radiation.

changed the way in which the sheets were folded to reduce folding time. However, bed making then took longer and couldn't be done easily if the patient was in the bed. The new methodology was abandoned—clearly early communication could have averted the frustration felt by all.

b. Quick wins are identified. This results in immediate gratification. For example, you could ensure that all departments have a copy of the names of patients coming to their department that day *and* a master list of appointments to help staff know where the patients are coming from and going to. Developing a communication strategy to highlight possible delays meant that patients who could be delayed by waiting for physicians were taken directly to the treatment area. Their chemotherapy started and the physician visit occurred in that area. This was expanded to appointment lists for two to three days ahead to facilitate planning.

c. Long-term improvements are identified that require a change in behavior, staffing, or course of action. The process may need committee approval or special funding. For example, you might have to purchase a new centrifuge in the lab so that specimens do not have to be batched in a large batch, or you might extend hours of operation. This needs planning to ensure both patient and staff goals are met.

3. The usual process is mapped but the exceptions to the rule are also mapped, depending on frequency. This creates opportunities to improve a process and prepare staff for all events. For example, at one of the U.S. sites, 16 percent of the patients coming for their outpatient chemotherapy or other infusion treatments were unscheduled or a walk-in. The team recognized that there will always be walk-ins, and understood that it is critical to know how to deal with these patients. However, they all felt the volume of walk-ins was too high and realized that many patients left without setting up their next appointment with a scheduler. This led to a blitz event, with all staff tasked with asking the patients if they had their next appointment; if they did not, they invited a scheduler to pop in and see them before they left the area. This led to an increased awareness of staff and patients, and the number of walk-ins dropped to 5 percent.

Implementing the Changes

Initially, the process mapping is discussed and the team is involved in reviewing and walking through the existing or new processes. Aptium then ensures the new or alternative process is thoroughly communicated. This includes involving patients, if appropriate. At our centers in the United States, we often used posters placed in strategic areas such as waiting rooms to announce changes to a process.

Patient safety is always the overarching theme in healthcare. Developing a culture of no blame is a principle fostered by Aptium. Accidents happen and Aptium recognizes that no one comes to work intending to make a mistake.

The following Lean principles are used to create an environment conducive to safe and efficient practice:

1. By using 5S, all departments are challenged to sort out not just their processes, but also their physical environment. Members of staff were encouraged to use this opportunity to move furniture and create a safe and pleasing environment, which could include removal of excess furniture or supplies. For example, one of our infusion areas always looked cluttered; there were also more slips and falls reported in this area than in any other department. The team working in the area was charged with finding a solution. It established that because staffing levels allowed no more than fifteen patients to be treated at any given time, the thirty available recliners were posing a problem. By removing fifteen recliners and replacing them with smaller visitors' chairs, the area became easier to move through and to keep clean and tidy. Once the environment is in order, staff find it easy to maintain their space. Standardizing the above process involved writing some policy and procedures on who was treated in chairs and who was treated in beds. It also involved making sure patients' visitors knew the new rules about chairs, so that they knew which chairs they could sit in. This resulted in signage much like you see on a bus: "You can sit here but may have to move if a patient needs the chair." Sustaining the process involves ongoing monitoring. Is the new process being followed? Is it working? Are fifteen chairs still enough or are more needed?
2. To reinforce the use of the 5S methodology and also to maintain an environment that meets all regulatory requirements, the facility

manager at our treatment centers performs a monthly safety round on a randomly selected day. It involves staff from various levels, and a thorough evaluation is conducted. This creates a learning experience for staff. The team of four could involve the facilities manager, a care support worker, a nurse, and an infection control guru one month, and the next month it could comprise the manager, a pharmacist, a finance person, and a porter. The team documents any deficiencies and the department is given a fixed period to remedy any problems. We found this to be a very valuable learning tool because it creates a window into other departments for the various team members. It also exposes them to different regulations and an increased awareness of their environment. We were fortunate to have management buy-in for this and all Lean processes.

3. At Aptium, all unexpected events trigger a Kaizen event. All Kaizen events are used as improving organization process (IOP) opportunities. The dashboard shown in Figure 2.1 is one of the tools used to document changes that may be needed. Most patient-related events will result in a root-cause analysis. Tools such as the Pareto chart are used to gather the information and develop an appropriate solution. Those are extreme opportunities to implement changes, but we also use our routine patient satisfaction surveys to identify opportunities for improvement. Management holds monthly meetings where staff at all levels are able to present storyboards or dashboards that reflect new processes or changes.

4. In developing an efficient model that achieves the goals identified, staffing numbers, staff roles, and patient education are critical. Another example from one of our sites in the United States shows how quick wins make a significant impact that can lead to other changes and greater efficiencies. The stocking of supply cabinets in the clinic area was carried out by nursing assistants (clinical support workers) throughout the day. When they were busy with restocking duties, registered nurses performed the assistants' duties as well as their own. The quick win involved developing par levels for all supplies with Kanbans that triggered a phone call to the storeroom if a particular item was running low. The storeroom clerk went to all three areas before clinic and stocked to the par level. The new process saved time and money. This small project led to more work, as the team involved in the process review was

multidisciplinary. Information was gathered on electronic supply cabinets with computer-generated inventory control and billing. The investment quickly paid off once electronic supply cabinets were placed in all areas. They were simple to use with minimal training and reduced the effort needed in inventory management and billing, and provided excellent storage space—definitely a win–win situation.

RESULTS AND LESSONS LEARNED

Continually Review the Process

Lean is a journey, not a destination. Lean principles stimulate continuous evaluation and change, with value creation always at the focus under the umbrella of safety. Some perceived efficiencies may create an unsafe or potentially unsafe environment. These problems are sometimes seen during the implementation phase, but sometimes they are identified only after the fact.

Ongoing education on Lean principles is reserved for those with problems accepting or understanding the process. We found that as Lean was absorbed, a culture developed and it was necessary to review the basics only with the new staff. Part of the culture of excellence that Lean promotes requires the development of an environment of learning—developing best practice based on the evidence seen. Exposure to new ideas, new equipment, and new software fosters the desire to stick with the journey and creates a happy staff.

Aptium uses several Lean techniques to monitor ongoing successes and adjust for potential failures:

1. All changes are documented and measured by using the IOP process. A dashboard for the change is implemented. This creates a visual tool for documenting and measuring changes. IOP also involves a monthly meeting for reporting back on key changes to all the stakeholders (i.e., management and co-workers). Some Aptium centers require all staff to participate in at least one IOP event a year, which helps sustain the Lean culture.

2. The Ohno circle is another technique used, where one person is assigned a day of observing departmental processes and tasked with coming up with suggestions for improvements. For example, after being in the Ohno circle, a nurse aide recognized that although patients were anxious about their next visit, they were leaving without making a future appointment. Problems were created when patients failed to come for their next visit or arrived but were not expected. The solution the team came up with was to implement a "roving scheduler" who at least hourly walked through the area where patients received their chemotherapy. Booking appointments fixed the problem and improved efficiency and patient satisfaction.

3. Staff job descriptions and annual goals and objectives have a Lean focus. New ideas are applauded and involvement in change is expected.

Embracing Lean

Earlier, we mentioned that Lean is all about mapping the end-to-end process. In fact, it is more than that. It is about embracing the process, learning from co-workers, and running with the change that best fits today, while never losing sight of the potential for tomorrow. It is teamwork at its best and it always results in value.

Aptium has been on a journey of improvement for more than twenty years. Lean provides a dynamic process that enables us to deliver effective and efficient care in a sustainable manner. It provides the tools we use for startups or consultancy projects. We depend on the principles outlined in this chapter to create and sustain our clinical and business model.

3

Providing Rapid Access to a Vascular Surgery Outpatient Clinic

Simon Dodds
Good Hope Hospital, Sutton Coldfield, U.K.

PROJECT BACKGROUND

In the summer of 1999, I started work as a newly appointed consultant vascular surgeon at Good Hope Hospital, a district general hospital situated at the northeast corner of the West Midlands region. Good Hope is a typical 500+ bed district general hospital that serves a mixed urban–rural population, delivering a broad range of outpatient and inpatient services.

My appointment was part of an expansion of the vascular surgery department in response to a steady increase in demand for specialist vascular surgical services. What I inherited was a conventional National Health Service (NHS) outpatient service with historically long waiting times, dedicated but overstretched staff, shabby facilities, and patients who had long since given up complaining and whose expectations were low.

As soon as I started at Good Hope Hospital it was clear to me that there were problems in the vascular surgery outpatient clinic—specifically, long waits for appointments, long delays for tests, long delays for review clinic visits, long waits in the clinic itself, and then long waits for treatment. No one was happy about the situation and no one seemed able to do anything about it. It was always someone else's fault. The layout of the clinic was also far from ideal for the staff and the patients, with long narrow corridors lined with chairs (Figure 3.1).

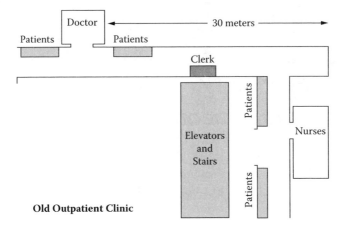

FIGURE 3.1
Schematic layout of the original vascular surgery outpatient clinic. Patients without chronic wounds waited outside the doctor's room; patients with chronic wounds were seen by the specialist nurses (and the doctor).

IMPLEMENTING LEAN

Identifying the Problem

The group of patients who seemed to fare the worst were the elderly, frail patients with chronic leg ulcers. Following a team-wide Strengths Weaknesses Opportunities Threats (SWOT) session, we agreed collectively to try to address some of the issues. Our shared vision was clear: rapid access to a high-quality and efficient outpatient service run by experienced and enthusiastic people and supported with the latest tools and technology. What was not so clear was what we were going to do to achieve our vision.

We started working on fixing what we could fix. There was no steering group, no project plan, no business case, no budget, and only occasional ad hoc meetings, usually held at the start or end of a clinic. However, it was clear that it was not the people who worked in the clinic who were the problem; it was the process that they were trying to work with. So we started challenging and changing the process (Figure 3.2).

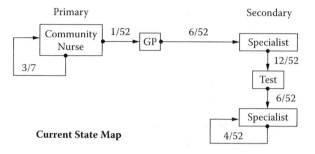

FIGURE 3.2

High-level value stream map (VSM) for a patient with a leg ulcer. The patient typically visits the community nurse every three days, and after twelve weeks is referred via the general practitioner to the specialist clinic. The conventional clinic is arranged as a new-test review process after which the patient is also reviewed in clinic every four weeks to assess response to treatment. The lead time from presentation to diagnosis is thirty-seven weeks (12 + 1 + 6 + 12 + 6 = 37).

First Cycle of Change (1999–2000)

First, we challenged the conventional new test review model of care. Why couldn't we do the test in the clinic? All that was needed for most patients was an ultrasound scan that took only a few minutes to perform, albeit by a vascular technologist using a sophisticated (yet mobile) duplex ultrasound machine. The time it took for a patient to be referred to the radiology department and return for his or her results was around eighteen weeks.

Why did patients have to wait eighteen weeks for a scan that took ten minutes to perform? So we asked the radiology people if they would come to the clinic with their ultrasound machine. There was initially some resistance to our suggestion. However, when we showed the number of patients who needed scans, it became apparent that coming to the clinic was just as good a use of their time and it would save them a lot of extra administrative work. There was potentially something in the suggested approach for everyone: the patient, the people in clinic, and the radiology department.

The change took place in June 2000; it cost nothing, and it slashed eighteen weeks off patient waiting times overnight. The change had other beneficial knock-on effects, too. It improved continuity of care in clinic; it reduced the number of letters that had to be dictated and typed; and it reduced the number of follow-up visits that were needed. The changes freed clinic time that could be reinvested in seeing new patients and reduced the time from referral to treatment. The change cost nothing other than a bit of negotiation.

Second Cycle of Change (2001–2003)

Following the implementation of the one-stop clinic, the next big complaint on our list was the poor communication we had with the district nurses who worked in the general practitioner (GP) practices and community-based clinics. It was the community nurses who provided the majority of the care for patients with leg ulcers, and they too experienced considerable problems in communicating with the specialist wound care nurses based at the hospital.

Again, it was not the people who caused the problem; it was the process. The common outcome was a late or at least delayed referral of patients, with the result that the ulcer was often very advanced and therefore more complex, time-consuming, and costly to treat. Difficult communication also often led to inappropriate treatment. Patients were confused because they were getting different messages and advice from different people. Again, we focused our attention on the process and took up the second challenge—to improve the communication.

This was a much tougher challenge because we had to design, test, and implement a new form of communication—a shared electronic patient record (EPR). It would include color digital images and would enable people to measure the size of the ulcer from the image. We wanted to be able to make accurate measurements of ulcer size and communicate these in the form of a graph to everyone who was involved in the care of the patient—in effect, a run chart of ulcer size. This was because we needed to be able to monitor the response to treatment and to change treatment only when we had objective evidence that the current treatment was not working. We used the PDCA (Plan Do Check Act) cycle in the form of a formal research trial—a carefully conducted experiment that would compare the current state of the communication process with the proposed future state. The leg ulcer telemedicine trial took us two years to complete.

The measured results were dramatic—an improvement in outcome (i.e., effectiveness) measured as an increase in the number of ulcers healed at twelve weeks from 38 to 64 percent. The time from referral to clinic was reduced from forty-one days to twelve days, and the cost of treatment

FIGURE 3.3
High-level VSM for the leg ulcer value stream after two cycles of change: first the development of the one-stop clinic and, second, the shared electronic patient record.

in the community was reduced by 26 percent. So the improvements were threefold: quality, timeliness, and cost.

Again, we had demonstrated improvements on all dimensions by focusing on improving the process; identifying what was getting in the way; and either removing it or replacing it with something better. It appeared that the less complicated the process became, the better it worked (Figure 3.3).

This second change had other beneficial knock-on effects. It allowed us to monitor the progress of the patient's treatment remotely without having to review the patient in clinic repeatedly. Previously, these extra visits were in effect rework because the community nurses were already seeing the patients regularly. Patients with chronic wounds represent a high and increasing demand for specialist services and, if those services are limited, then the delays this creates translate to poorer outcomes and increased costs of treatment—the lose–lose–lose scenario. By simply improving communication, we had made a significant improvement on all dimensions.

Following the successful pilot of the leg ulcer telemedicine (LUTM) service, we were surprised and delighted to learn that the community nurse teams who had been involved in the trial did not want to go back to "the dark ages" and wanted to continue to use the new communication medium. The prototype system was then developed to a commercial-grade product and rolled out to all community nurse teams across the locality.

The measured impact on the number of clinic visits for patients with leg ulcers is shown in the run chart in Figure 3.4. Even without any statistical analysis, the reduction in number of follow-up visits is clearly visible.

A Pause to Celebrate (2004)

It was about this time that our work came to the attention of people outside our organization, and we were advised to submit our work for the NHS

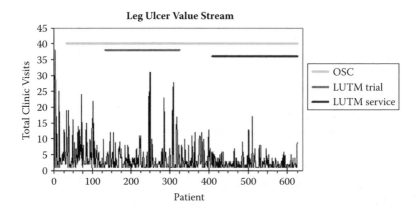

FIGURE 3.4

Run chart of the total number of outpatient clinic visits for individual patients with leg ulcers. It clearly shows a reduction in outpatient visits associated with the roll out of the LUTM service, which improved the communication process between the community-based and hospital-based nurses.

Innovation Awards. It was even more exciting to actually win the Innovation Award for Service Improvement and to gain national recognition for the work that the front-line team had done. It was also interesting to observe that, despite this award, our work did not attract any attention from the upper echelons of the NHS.

Third Cycle of Change (2004–2005)

The next niggle that made itself apparent related to the way the clinics themselves worked. By reducing the number of review patients, we released capacity to see more new patients with leg ulcers—patients who represented an unmet need, a hidden demand.

The problem this posed was that these patients were the most complex ones attending the one-stop clinic. A new patient with a leg ulcer required about ninety minutes to complete a full assessment, ultrasound scan, and review, and to start the wound care treatment. Increasing the proportion of new patients compared with the easier review of patients started to cause problems: the clinics were running over time in an unpredictable way and the specialist nurses were becoming stressed.

This was a different problem from the previous ones, and it was a lot more complex. The problem was caused by the demand for clinic time, which was variable both in number of appointments and complexity and, more specifically, a mismatch between this demand and the way that the clinic was scheduled. The clinic scheduling method had not changed for years and was still based on the historical generic "new" and "review" appointment slots. By changing the process, we had now highlighted that this method of scheduling was no longer fit for that purpose because it took no account of the variability and case mix. Clinic slots were filled in a first-come/first-served way. If a new leg ulcer was booked into the last new slot, then the clinic would overrun. What we needed was a clinic scheduling method that matched the clinic capacity more closely to the patient demand.

The approach I used was, with the benefit of hindsight, a well-used Lean Sigma method. First, I conducted a retrospective analysis of the demand in terms of case mix and found that there were actually only four categories of patients, according to their need for clinic resources: new leg ulcer, review leg ulcer, new vascular, and other. The process maps for each of these were quite different—ranging from just fifteen minutes with the doctor to ninety minutes and all the resources of the one-stop clinic (nurse, technologist, doctor, and treatment room). We followed a dozen or so of each category through the clinic and measured how long each step took. From this, we removed the steps where patients were waiting and calculated the average and the variance of the times of the remainder—in effect, the value-added work.

The next step was to design a booking schedule that better matched the demand to the capacity of each resource in the clinic, both in terms of volume and case mix—in effect, a booking timetable or template for the one-stop clinic. This was a significant challenge because of the high degree of variability from one patient to the next that our measurements had shown. This variability appeared to be a feature of the patient rather than a result of the process, so we needed to design a solution that was resilient to this variation without failing.

It was immediately apparent that there were a large number of ways of arranging the clinic bookings. However, it was not clear which approach would work and which would be the best. If we got it wrong, then we could make the problem worse rather than better.

What I needed to be able to do was to test our proposed options for a new booking schedule and obtain objective evidence of the performance of each one. From that, we could choose the best approach and present the evidence that it would work before implementing it.

I was vaguely aware of the academic discipline known as operational research (OR), which I thought looked at this sort of problem. However, I could find very little evidence of examples of successful and sustained implementations in healthcare. I suspected that the methods derived from and applied to industrial processes were not immediately applicable to healthcare, because of the high degree of patient-to-patient variability. Even knowing quite a lot about a patient before the patient arrives in clinic, the on-the-spot problem-solving approach required for complex medical problems does not translate easily to a Lean process. We needed a solution that was both quick and resilient.

Fortunately, my previous experience with computer modeling of complex vascular flow networks was very helpful in solving this problem. The difference was that individual patients do not "flow" through a clinic in the same way that blood flows in an artery. The clinic process looks like a series of gates that open and close to allow a patient through to the next step. To simulate this sort of process requires a different tool known as discrete event simulation (DES). I knew this because I had used DES before when I simulated data flows through a computer system as part of a system optimization exercise.

A model is a simplified representation of reality and for a process there are three components to the model:

- The work list of patients, which represents the demand (input)
- The resources available, which represent the capacity (input)
- The pathway, which represents the value stream (transformation)

With enough detail, it would be possible to simulate the outpatient clinic and generate some outputs—predictions of how the system would perform over a range of realistic operating conditions. In fact, we already had this information because we had looked at our historical demand and case mix, identified the product lines, and mapped and measured the streams. Therefore, we knew what resources we had. Unfortunately, none of the commercially available DES tools met my requirements—simple to use, cheap, accurate, and flexible. As a result, I used a very simple DES tool that I had written many years previously, and adapted it for the purpose.

All I needed to do was to test the proposed booking options and predict how each would perform in terms of clinic finish time, patient waiting time, and balance of work across all the resources in clinic. The option that showed predictable and acceptable clinic finish times, predictable and acceptable waiting times, and a predictable and acceptable balance of work would be a viable solution. In retrospect, what I was looking for was a design that would deliver a process that was in statistical control and capable of meeting the specification. I didn't know that then because I had not heard of the work of Walter Shewhart and W. Edwards Deming. What I did not want was a sophisticated tool that would search for the optimum solution. I knew from my computer science training that finding the optimum is a hard task—similar to programming a computer to play a good game of chess. I didn't need the computer to be creative; I simply needed to test the options and predict how they would perform.

Once all the pieces were in place, the actual work of building and testing the model and comparing the options took only a couple of days. The final output was a new booking schedule that met the design constraints in terms of clinic finish time, patient waiting time, and workload balance. It also predicted a 40 percent increase in maximum clinic capacity in terms of the number of patients that could be seen—from sixteen to twenty-two patients.

This result was surprising and emerged because the pathways of individual patients interweaved in an elegant "dance" with each other and the available resources. The new schedule was implemented very simply as a printed schedule. All the clinic clerk had to do was to match each patient booking with the next free slot in the schedule of that category to get the starting time, and then make bookings in the patient administration system (PAS) for individual resources schedules such as for the doctor, nurse, and technologist.

The new design was actually a set of interwoven first-in/first-out (FIFO) queues. It was obvious from looking at the booking sheets if any particular stream was flowing. In retrospect, we had designed a simple visual system for both managing and monitoring the process. However, at the time, I hadn't heard of visual reporting.

The new schedule was piloted late in 2004 (Figure 3.5), and the subsequent audit showed that the clinic behaved just as predicted by the value stream model. Even when booked to maximum capacity, the clinic was busy but not frantic, and still finished on time. The informal feedback

Mr. S.R. Dodds One-Stop Outpatient Clinic GHH Booking Template										
Day	Wednesday									
Time	14.00–17.00									
Date										
Version 18/12/2003							A38	E16	E17	E16
#	Time	Patient Type	Number	Surname	Forename	DOB	Cons	CNS	V-Lab	Dress
1	14:00	New Leg Ulcer						14:00	15:00	15:30
2	14:00	FU Leg Ulcer								14:00
3	14:00	FU Leg Ulcer								14:00
4	14:00	New Vascular					14:00		14:15	
5	14:15	New/FU					14:15			
6	14:30	New Leg Ulcer						14:30	15:30	16:00
7	14:30	FU Leg Ulcer								14:30
8	14:30	New Vascular					14:30		14:45	
9	14:45	New/FU					14:45			
10	15:00	New Leg Ulcer						15:00	16:00	16:30
11	15:00	FU Leg Ulcer								15:00
12	15:00	New Vascular					15:00		15:15	
13	15:15	New/FU					15:15			
14	15:30	New Vascular					15:30		15:45	
15	15:30	FU Leg Ulcer								15:30
16	15:45	New/FU					15:45			
17	16:00	URG Dressing								16:00
18	16:00	URG Dressing								16:00
19	16:00	New Vascular					16:00		16:15	
20	16:15	New/FU					16:15			
21	16:30	New/FU					16:30			
22	16:45	New/FU					16:45			

FIGURE 3.5

Reproduction of the original redesigned one-stop clinic booking schedule that balanced demand with capacity, taking into account the inevitable variation in the process to deliver consistent and acceptable performance.

from the staff was that it just seemed to run better and that the days of late finishes, missed lunch breaks, and frustrated patients appeared to be in the past. The increased maximum capacity created by the redesigned template meant that the clinic had enough resilience to absorb the inevitable variation in demand, such as urgent requests. Once again, it appeared that we had achieved another win–win–win outcome.

The Fourth Cycle of Change (2005)

All the changes outlined so far occurred in the old outpatient clinic and, even with this inconvenient layout, we achieved significant improvements in the quality and performance of the process; all without any significant financial investment.

However, in September 2005 we moved to a new treatment center that had been built at Good Hope Hospital. As part of this initiative, we had the opportunity to influence the layout of the clinical area we were to move to. This allowed us to build on the work we had already done and, in collaboration with the architects, we designed the new layout (Figure 3.6).

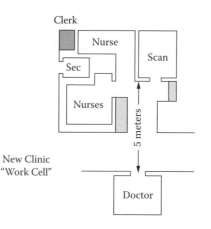

FIGURE 3.6

Schematic layout of the new one-stop vascular clinic. The co-location of the doctors, nurses, and technologists in a work cell design ensures that everyone can move quickly from one room to another. Combined with the level schedule, there is almost no need for a waiting room. I subsequently learned that we had, in effect, designed a work cell that reduced the transport and motion waste inherent in the original clinic.

Multiskilling

Since moving to the new facility, we have implemented further incremental changes. For example, we have acquired a second mobile ultrasound machine, which means a consultant, with some extra training, can now perform some of the less complex scans. This eliminates some hand-offs and delays, and is particularly useful if the vascular technologist is busy with complex patients. It has resulted in an improvement in the waiting times for patients and has demonstrated the resilience of the design.

Today's Work Today

The most recent improvement has been to bring the secretary down to the clinic so that letters are typed on the same day. To implement this improvement, the doctor now dictates the letter immediately after the patient has left, and passes the notes and tape to the secretary. The secretary then types the letter and returns it for checking and signing. At the end of the clinic's day, the completed letters are put in the post and the notes are returned to the medical records library. This eliminates the transport of the notes to and from the secretary's office. The GP receives the clinic letter within twenty-four hours, and patients can take a copy of their letter if they wait a few more minutes after seeing the doctor. Doctors can check the letter when the patient is still fresh in their mind. All provide immediate opportunities to identify and correct any mistakes.

RESULTS AND LESSONS LEARNED

The implementation of the one-stop clinic reduced patient waiting times by eighteen weeks. It also reduced administration time (dictating and typing letters; organizing follow-up visits) in the clinic. And it improved the continuity of care.

The introduction of the LUTM system resulted in a much simpler process that improved the quality, efficiency, and cost of the service. The number of ulcers healed at twelve weeks increased, the time from referral to clinic was reduced, and the cost of treatment was reduced.

The improved booking schedule enabled us to match each type of patient booking with the available resources in that category. Although the clinic was still busy, the work flowed much more smoothly.

The acquisition of a second mobile ultrasound machine has cut out some delays and hand-offs, and so has reduced waiting times for patients.

Moving the secretary down to the clinic has also cut out some hand-offs, because notes no longer need to be passed from the clinic to the secretary's office.

Our experience demonstrates that the principles of value stream investigation (VSI) apply in healthcare just as they do in other areas such as manufacturing and service industries. It is not necessary to adopt a regimented "out of the box" approach to this.

However, the following core principles must be clearly understood:

- Strive continuously to improve the quality and cost-effectiveness as viewed by the customer—at every point in the value system
- Respect all the people involved in achieving this

Once these core values are made explicit, agreed, practiced, and if necessary enforced, then (and only then) can the tools and techniques of Lean be applied. Once these skills are acquired and embedded, the more sophisticated data-driven tools of Six Sigma can be used.

Finally, when the attitude, skills, and knowledge are embraced, the emerging combination of the art and science of value stream design (VSD) can then be employed.

Everything I have learned and experienced in the last eight years leads me to conclude that we are on the cusp of an exciting period of positive change in healthcare. The win–win–win era has arrived!

4

Reorganizing and Standardizing Supply Rooms across a Health System

Franciscan Health System, Puget Sound, Washington

PROJECT BACKGROUND

The Lean program at Franciscan Health System (FHS) is managed by the Lean program manager, Karl Kraber, who has been responsible for initiating Lean throughout the five-hospital system. His activities are overseen by the Lean Executive Steering Committee (LESC), which selects and sponsors the regional Lean activities for FHS. The LESC consists of twenty-one members, including the five hospital chief operating officers (COOs) and departmental vice presidents. Once a regional project has been selected, one of the LESC executives serves as a sponsor to provide authority to the project.

The first responsibility of the sponsor is to select a management guidance team (MGT), made up of directors and managers who own the process and departments affected by the Lean project. This team provides the guidance, resources, and insights needed by the team to be effective. With input from the MGT, the sponsor then identifies the leader and members to improve the process selected (Figure 4.1).

Background Issues

In the fall of 2007, the LESC wanted to know what hospital managers and staff thought were the most pressing problems affecting productivity and efficiency in their areas. As a result, 100 managers and staff in both the clinical and ancillary departments were interviewed. The resulting

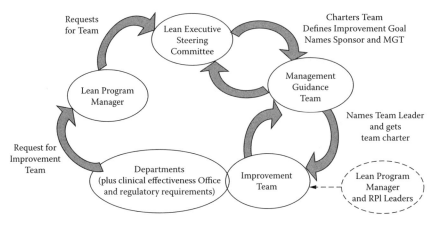

FIGURE 4.1
Lean selection and reporting structure.

Pareto chart (Figure 4.2) shows that "supplies and equipment" was the main area of opportunity for improvement. The problem was that front-line caregivers could not quickly and easily find the supplies and equipment needed to provide patient care.

The central supply room was the one area common to all clinical departments, so the LESC decided that supply rooms should be reorganized and standardized across FHS in an effort to improve availability to staff. The Lean method that was selected for this improvement opportunity was 5S. The project came to be known simply as Regional 5S.

The Lean Tools Used

The 5S acronym *as we use it* stands for Sort, Simplify, Sweep, Standardize, and Sustain. It is sometimes referred to as a housekeeping methodology, which is misleading because organizing a workplace goes beyond housekeeping.

Recognizing that supply rooms were not the only source of frustration and wasted time, the LESC decided to attack this problem in three major phases. This chapter concentrates on the first phase of the Regional 5S project.

The three phases of the Regional 5S project were as follows:

- Phase 1 took place in the patient care units. It aimed to standardize across all of FHS the grouping of supplies into major color categories to make finding supplies easier and faster—no matter which unit or hospital they are in (Figure 4.3). This phase occurred in 2008.

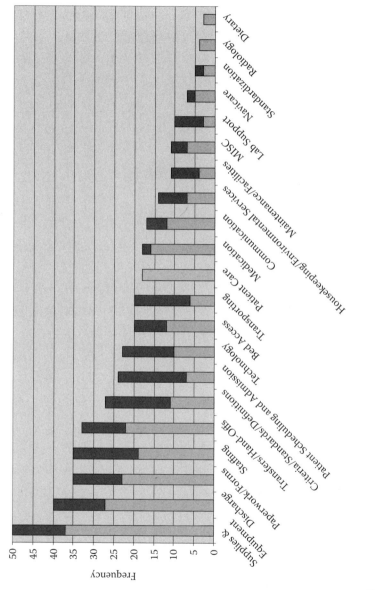

FIGURE 4.2
Pareto chart of improvement opportunities. Both groups (patient care units and all others) are combined.

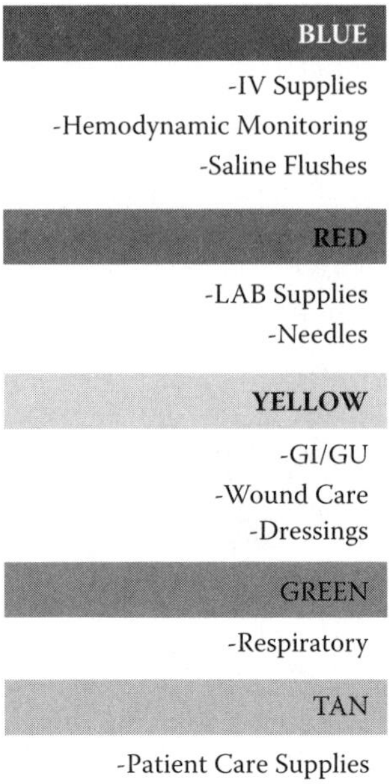

BLUE
-IV Supplies
-Hemodynamic Monitoring
-Saline Flushes

RED
-LAB Supplies
-Needles

YELLOW
-GI/GU
-Wound Care
-Dressings

GREEN
-Respiratory

TAN
-Patient Care Supplies

FIGURE 4.3
Color-coded categories for supply items.

- In Phase 2, each patient care unit is to expand the application of 5S to other areas of their choosing within their unit.
- Phase 3 will standardize the location and usage of shared hospital equipment that is not owned by specific units. This includes patient monitors, IV pumps and poles, beds, and so on.

IMPLEMENTING LEAN

Phase 1

The Lean program manager created a fifteen-minute video on 5S, called "5S at FHS." By using the St. Joseph Medical Center pharmacy as the case study, the "5S at FHS" video highlighted the value of doing 5S, described what it is, and outlined how to implement it.

Alison Roberts (then clinical support coordinator of the St. Joseph Medical Center critical care unit) was required to do a process improvement project as part of a group project while she was a senior nursing student at Pacific Lutheran University in the summer of 2007. This group of senior nursing students included another critical care employee, Karen Montejano, who along with Alison was in a unique position to support this project implementation by working in the unit where the event occurred.

The group started by researching several business and nursing articles to better understand Lean principles, and how they were applied in different contexts, especially in healthcare. The group also studied the principles of 5S and decided on a systematic approach to organizing the central supply areas. The result was the development of the five color-coded categories.

A 5S team was created from employees in Critical Care, representing both shifts and including nurses and care assistants. Alison Roberts served as the unit champion (UC) and facilitated this unit 5S team. She held several meetings in preparation for Sort day—the day of changing the supply system on the unit. This has since come to be known as the 5S event day. During these meetings, the group decided how to apply the color-coded supply system categorized by the function of the actual supply item. All medical and patient care supplies were then categorized into the five colors, based on how they were used. Colored bins were purchased in several sizes. Wire shelving was already installed in the supply areas, so cost was minimal.

The 5S event day in Critical Care occurred on June 19, 2007. Employees from the critical care 5S team as well as ancillary departments, such as respiratory therapists and materials management staff, physically categorized thousands of supplies into the color-coded system. Stocking levels were adjusted, and items most frequently used were placed at shelf levels that did not require reaching or bending. Two large supply rooms were converted on that day.

The color-coded system was visually defining, and was structured so that like-items were stocked next to like-items. For example, all bathing products were stocked in the same location in tan bins. All items used in point-of-care testing were grouped in red bins. This included items such as lab tubes, culturettes, cotton balls, and lancets. All the color-coded bins were then labeled with clear, large tape labels. This enabled staff to easily identify the product for which they were searching and helped the person stocking to easily work out where to place the product.

FIGURE 4.4
The supply room in Critical Care using the new color-coded system.

Posters were printed, laminated, and placed in the supply areas to reinforce the new color system. This served as a reference for anyone entering the supply room to obtain a product. Large butcher block paper was placed on the wall, asking staff for feedback. We did this because we wanted to know whether supplies had accidentally dropped off our profiles, if our stocking levels were adequate, if the color itemizing was logical and accurate, and any other feedback that they wanted to share with us. This project was meant to improve their workflow and satisfaction regarding finding supplies, and we wanted all staff to feel as if they had a voice in the final product. This feedback was then brought back to the unit's 5S team to evaluate and determine whether supply levels needed to be adjusted or if bins needed to be relocated within the room. Figure 4.4 shows how one of the critical care supply rooms looked after the Sort day.

Once the supply areas in Critical Care were transformed using the new color-coded system, we included before-and-after photos in a presentation given to all 200 unit employees. Because one of the major 5S principles is Sustain, a Microsoft PowerPoint presentation was developed to describe the 5S process and how Critical Care transformed its supply areas; this presentation is now given to all newly hired employees in Critical Care.

Planning and Preparation for Other Units

With the color-coded system defined, a video in hand, and direction from the LESC to conduct 5S in each inpatient care unit, the next step was deciding when each unit would hold its 5S event. We had learned a big lesson the previous year in trying to schedule Lean activities too soon after an area for improvement had been selected. The result was that it was hard to get team members to attend the improvement events. Consequently, we decided to let each unit do 5S at its convenience to allow it to fit the events into staff work schedules, with the caveat that it had to be done in 2008.

To ensure that a project of this magnitude would be successful, a schematic was created to define the roles and responsibilities and to help participants visualize the cascading nature of the plan (Figure 4.5). Since sustaining the outcomes of process improvement efforts has long been our Achilles heel, we created a structure to support 5S implementation and sustain it.

The first group to be identified and selected was the hospital 5S champions (HCs). The HCs were the "keepers of the color-coded categories." They were responsible for ensuring that the clinical units put and kept the supply items in the appropriate categories. They also acted as advisors to the unit 5S champions (UCs) and their respective nursing units and to the Lean program manager before, during, and after the 5S events.

The second group identified was the UCs. They, along with their managers, were responsible for ensuring that everyone in the department viewed the "5S at FHS" video prior to the 5S event day. They helped to select team members, oversaw the planning and logistics of the 5S event, and then led the team through the 5S event day. The UCs were among the most significant players, as they were the primary contact for the HCs and Lean program manager before, during, and after the 5S event.

The 5S team members—who would do the sorting, simplifying, and sweeping on the day of the event—consisted of representatives from as many areas, functions, and specialties in the unit as possible. Whoever was affected by the change was invited to participate on the team. The central supply representatives (CSRs) were also invited to help with relabeling the supply bins and adjusting the par level for items in our computerized supply system.

The next group defined was the Regional 5S Sustain Team. This team consisted of the HCs and UCs, and was led by the Lean program manager.

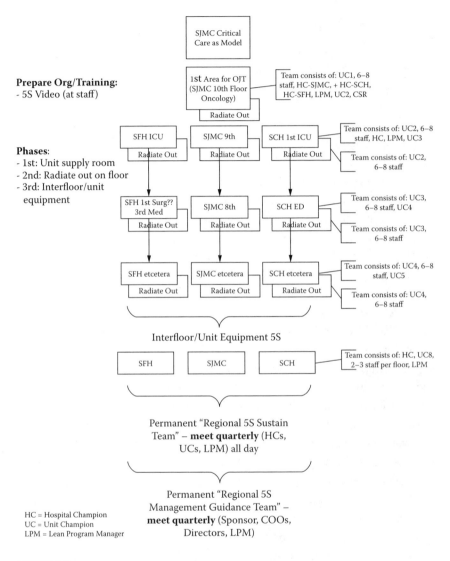

Prepare Org/Training:
- 5S Video (at staff)

Phases:
- 1st: Unit supply room
- 2nd: Radiate out on floor
- 3rd: Interfloor/unit equipment

HC = Hospital Champion
UC = Unit Champion
LPM = Lean Program Manager

FIGURE 4.5

Regional 5S for patient care units.

Its purpose was to discuss and resolve regionwide issues, to share lessons learned, to advise the Lean program manager on how to ensure successful implementation, and to learn more about 5S and visual control to advance the use of this Lean method. For example, at one meeting, we discussed the fact that there were units using department-specific supplies, such as peritoneal dialysis care. Instead of separating dozens of items for this diagnosis into five different colored bins, the group decided that these types of supplies could be grouped together and placed into orange bins. This allowed for separation from the main supply chain, but grouped them together logically for ease in finding for hospital staff.

The Regional 5S Management Guidance Team (5S MGT) consisted of the clinical managers, directors, COOs, and the executive sponsor of the Regional 5S project. They met with the Regional 5S sustain team to ensure standardization across the hospitals, resolve cross-functional authority issues, and to provide requested guidance to the units.

Once Critical Care transformed its supply areas, Alison Roberts presented the unit's experience at a meeting with the 5S MGT. This enabled the sponsors of the project to see firsthand the transformation of the supply areas through the use of photos. It also meant that the experience could be shared and celebrated by those attending the meeting.

Training and Implementation

Once the 5S event date was chosen for a unit, the preparation began. There were two major components to the preparation:

1. The UC had to ensure that all the unit team members had been selected and the logistics planned.
2. Everyone in the department was informed and trained for the 5S event.

The Lean program manager met with the UC and their manager to write the charter. At that time, the UC was provided with an eight-hour agenda for the event, a materials checklist, and a tip sheet to help plan and conduct a successful event. The Lean program manager also attended the 5S events to provide any necessary coaching.

Everyone in the affected department was required to view the "5S at FHS" video. The reasons for viewing the video were twofold:

- To ensure that everyone knew what was about to happen so that all could support (or at least not interfere with) the 5S effort
- To train those participating in the 5S effort on what would be expected of them

The video was provided in three formats for ease of use: DVD, VHS, and online.

RESULTS AND LESSONS LEARNED

Figure 4.6 shows the before-and-after pictures from one of the units that has implemented 5S. We quantified the before-and-after state of the supply rooms and staff attitudes by surveying the staff. Although we do not consider this to be a "scientific" study, it does give a good indication of the positive impact that doing 5S has had on the nursing staff. All units that conducted 5S were surveyed. Figure 4.7 through Figure 4.9 show some of the results of this survey.

Overall, we were pleased with the success of the project. Although it took some time for people to get used to the new shelf location of supplies, this was far outweighed by having everything well organized and easier to find. Change was difficult to accept for some staff, but after they learned the new system, they did find it to be more useful and better organized. We also learned that new staff adapted more quickly to the supply system than existing staff, as they did not have to "unlearn" and then "relearn."

The major challenges we face are ensuring that all the units have the items in their correct respective category, keeping items at their par levels, and integrating new products into the correct color-coded bin. One of the most significant challenges we still face today is the staff tendency to hoard supplies and equipment. Staff are so used to running out of items that they are now creating a self-fulfilling prophecy by their own behavior. In essence, what is occurring is that because of past experiences of supply outages or shortages, staff grab handfuls of product and stash them into secret cabinets or their pockets, or they overfill their unit's supply carts. This in turn can lead to increased supply usage and allows for products to expire because they are hidden away.

For 5S to be successful, our staff have to learn to trust the system that is in place for stocking supplies. Bins that are empty will be refilled automatically, based on their scheduled stocking time. If a critical item is out (as evidenced by an empty bin), staff can easily write down the number from the front of the bin, phone the supply department, and expect to receive it in a timely manner. If a new procedure is introduced or a new

(a)

(b)

FIGURE 4.6

St. Joseph Medical Center suture cabinet (a) before and (b) after 5S.

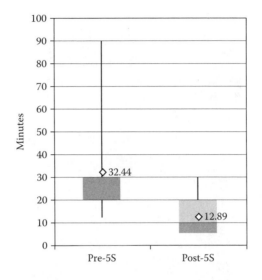

FIGURE 4.7
Answers to survey question, "How much time did you spend on your eight-hour shift looking for supplies?"

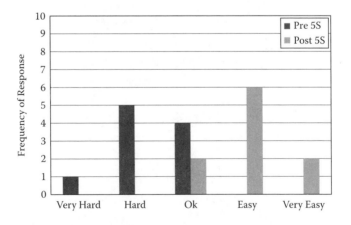

FIGURE 4.8
Survey response, rating overall satisfaction with supply organization.

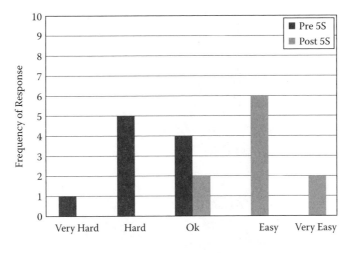

FIGURE 4.9
Survey response, rating how easy or hard it was to locate patient supplies.

product is requested from a physician, staff can give that feedback to their 5S team so that it can be incorporated into the color-coded system.

THE LEAN INITIATIVE THAT FOLLOWED

In October 2008, Critical Care continued implementing the color-coded system by radiating out to the supply cart in each patient care unit. Supplies were streamlined into color-coded categories, and now match the same system as the central supply area. This reinforces the 5S system throughout the entire unit. It not only makes it easier for staff to find products no matter where they are looking for them, it also helps the staff who are stocking products to do so in a consistent manner.

During the last Regional 5S Sustain Team meeting, we visited the units at two of the three participating hospitals. Our purpose for the visits was to see how each unit had implemented 5S and to do an impromptu survey of what worked and what did not work about using 5S in the supply rooms. Although everyone was required to use the color-coded categories and to have the right items in the right categories, staff were given latitude about how this was done. For example, some units chose to use colored bins for

FIGURE 4.10
Rehab supply locker using tape to demarcate the categories.

each category whereas other units used tape to demarcate the categories (see Figure 4.10 for an example of the use of tape).

We also learned that not all the units were doing necessary follow-up on issues that had been raised by staff, such as:

- Inability to see through packaging
- Too much stuff in too small a room
- Too many products in a bin without dividers
- Need for bigger labels
- Need for timelier stocking of supplies
- Inability to see small supplies behind bigger items
- Linen in supply rooms

We are trying to learn from our 5S experience as we apply Plan, Do, Check, Adjust (PDCA) to each of the units that has done 5S and each successive area. The challenges we have experienced have helped shape our approach and, in some instances, caused us to renegotiate roles and responsibilities on the floor and among the UCs and HCs. In addition, it has been necessary to learn from each other and understand our interdependencies. The success has increased acceptance of the overall Lean concept. This can be seen in the significant increase in requests for Lean events.

Overall, we are very pleased with the progress we've made and the success we've achieved. We believe that doing 5S had an immediate and significant positive impact on our clinical units.

5

A Quick-Start Lean Method to Cut the Clutter and Get Your Hospital Back into Shape

Kelley Williamson
University of Colorado Hospital, Denver, Colorado

PROJECT BACKGROUND

The University of Colorado Hospital is the region's leading specialty care and referral center. It is a family-focused hospital that offers patients the most advanced medical treatment and the finest amenities available. The first phase of the hospital included an intensive care unit, medical and surgical units, a clinical lab, pharmacy, private patient rooms, and family sleeping areas. The remaining phases were opened in June 2007. Primary care clinics are operated by the hospital in six convenient Denver metro locations.

Since 1992, there has been a continual move (unit by unit) from one campus location to another because of lack of space. Space is at a critical premium when running all the functions within a hospital facility, and even more so when a large hospital is moving from one campus to another. The 5S tool provided a solution to space issues without downsizing staff or incurring large-scale capital building costs.

A transition team was formed to develop and implement ways to remove paper waste, stationery supplies, biomedical supplies, and equipment waste from the hospital system before it was loaded onto tractor trailers and taken to the new location. The transition team sought outside ideas to design a plan to eliminate waste and increase employee engagement.

Problems to Address

One of the first steps in the 5S project was to survey employees to determine what issues they were experiencing around the move. They identified the following high-level issues:

- Low employee morale
  Reason: The employees felt that they were no longer involved in any decision-making processes that affected the financial stability of the hospital. This evolved after the hospital decided to:
  - Change campuses without explaining why it was not expanding
  - Locate and merge units that had never been together before
- Lower employee opinion scores than expected
  Reason: Over the past five years, the hospital has used employee opinion surveys. The low scores were attributed to the change and transition that employees were experiencing. Employees stated that they felt they had "little control" over what was happening.
- No process improvement initiatives
  Reason: Current management was and is involved in day-to-day administrative issues, which keeps it from focusing on process issues that have existed at the hospital for many years.

5S

The hospital chose 5S because it was a simple but highly effective set of techniques and tools that would help in the removal of waste from the work environment through better workplace organization, visual communication, and general cleanliness.

The five pillars of 5S are defined as Sort, Set in order, Shine, Standardize, and Sustain.

IMPLEMENTING LEAN

Naming the Project

After choosing 5S as the Lean tool to help the hospital, we held a contest for all employees to name the 5S project that was to be undertaken at the

University of Colorado Hospital. More than a hundred names and themes were submitted. After much debate, the 5S project was named "Clean Sweep—Out with the Old, In with the New to Become a More Efficient U."

With the move to the new campus quickly approaching, a fast and furious timeline was put in place to educate, train, and implement the 5S Clean Sweep project in a sixty-day timeframe.

Tools Used

We used a number of tools, techniques, and games in this very successful project (Figure 5.1).

Educating

During the sixty-day timeline, we needed to educate managers and train employees. We used a monthly transition committee meeting to update the managers.

At the first meeting, the following information was presented to the managers and directors:

- What 5S meant and how it would be implemented at the hospital
- Dates for the Clean Sweep events in 2006/2007
- Clean Sweep logo and poster design
- Requests to managers for volunteer employees, who would be the team leads during the Clean Sweep events

Measurements for End Results

The session with the managers and directors of the hospital was a great success. The Clean Sweep project was seen as a creative and engaging event that would involve all employees in cleaning up waste and creating a workplace that everyone would be proud to work in. The project was also praised because it would create a new standard for the hospital, both for the present and the future.

Training

The second phase was to train all employees. This involved creating a brochure about what 5S was and how it would be used in a hospital setting.

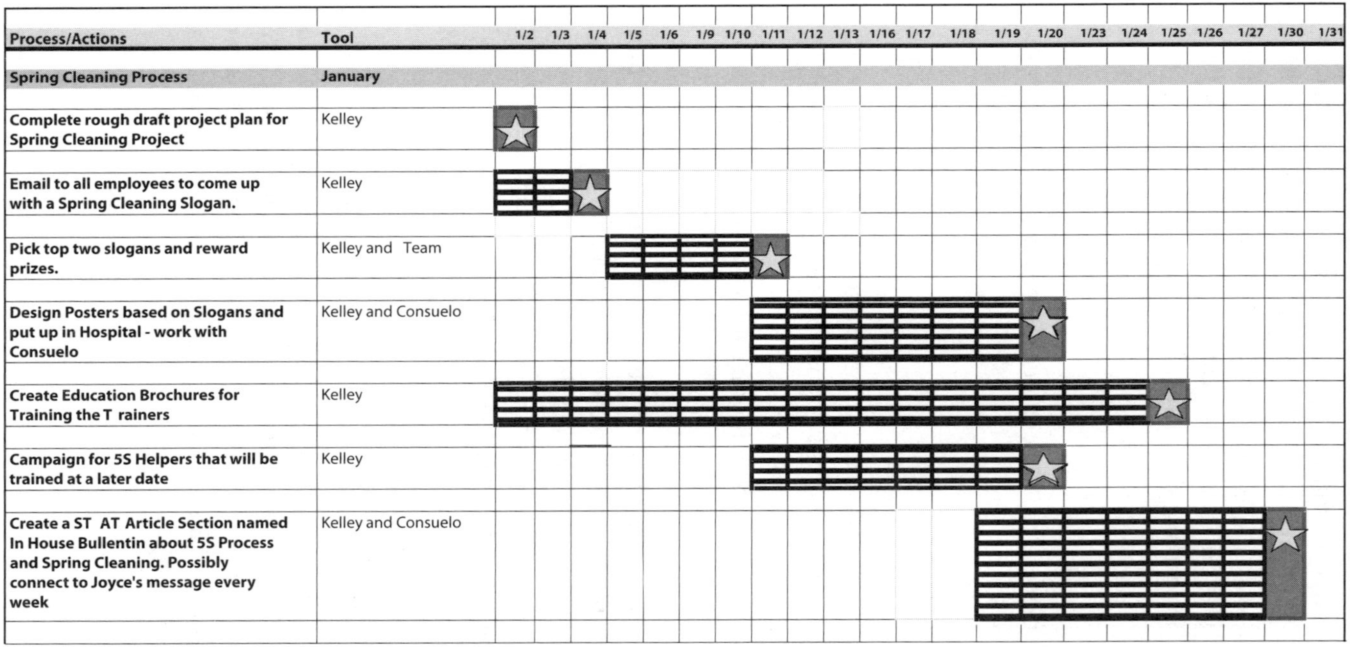

Process/Actions	Tool
Spring Cleaning Process	**January**
Complete rough draft project plan for Spring Cleaning Project	Kelley
Email to all employees to come up with a Spring Cleaning Slogan.	Kelley
Pick top two slogans and reward prizes.	Kelley and Team
Design Posters based on Slogans and put up in Hospital - work with Consuelo	Kelley and Consuelo
Create Education Brochures for Training the T rainers	Kelley
Campaign for 5S Helpers that will be trained at a later date	Kelley
Create a ST AT Article Section named In House Bullentin about 5S Process and Spring Cleaning. Possibly connect to Joyce's message every week	Kelley and Consuelo

Date columns: 1/2, 1/3, 1/4, 1/5, 1/6, 1/9, 1/10, 1/11, 1/12, 1/13, 1/16, 1/17, 1/18, 1/19, 1/20, 1/23, 1/24, 1/25, 1/26, 1/27, 1/30, 1/31

FIGURE 5.1

Tools, techniques, and games used in the project. Timeline: 60 days.

Process/Actions	Tool	1/2	1/3	1/4	1/5	1/6	1/9	1/10	1/11	1/12	1/13	1/16	1/17	1/18	1/19	1/20	1/23	1/24	1/25	1/26	1/27	1/30	1/31
Develop a game to have the first five people that can answer a queston found in ST AT bulletin will receive a cleaning pin or some other idea	Kelley																						
Begin taking pictures of the good and not so good of cleaning/offices/hidden rooms.	Kelley and Consuelo																						
Design steps for Blue T ag Strategy and Criteria	Kelley and Team																						
Send Blue T ags for Printing	Kelley and Kinkos																						
Create email blasts that are comical and follow slogan to market spring cleaning	Kelley and Consuelo																						
Meet with consolidation teams for where to place bins at docks etc. Make sure process is in place	Kelley and Team																						

can start ▭ rliest date on which action
▬ on which action must
complete ★ CRITICAL PATH

FIGURE 5.1 (continued)

Process/Actions	Tool	2/2	2/3	2/6	2/7	2/8	2/9	2/10	2/13	2/14	2/15	2/16	2/17	2/20	2/21	2/22	2/23	2/24	2/27	2/28
Spring Cleaning Process	**February**																			
Create the forms needed for Blue Tagging, uneeded equipment, etc	Kelley and Team	▮	▮	▮	▮	▮	▮	★												
Create a policies and procedures game with scenarios for train the trainer sessions to rollout at staff meetings	Kelley	▮	▮	▮	★															
Begin collecting stories on dollars saved, space saved, etc.	Kelley and Consuelo	▮	▮	▮	▮	▮	▮	▮	▮	▮	▮	▮	▮	▮	▮	▮	▮	▮	▮	▮
Formal letter from Joyce or Bruce to begin the process and get buyin.	Kelley and Candy					▮	★													
Design prize programs for oldest equipment, etc.	Kelley and Team										▮	▮	▮	▮	★					
Work with Environmental Services for cleaning readiness	Kelley and John										▮	▮	▮	▮	★					
Training Sessions for T rain the T rainer Volunteers	Kelley and Team										▮	▮	▮	▮	★					

FIGURE 5.1 (continued)

Process/Actions	Tool	1/2	1/3	1/4	1/5	1/6	1/9	1/10	1/11	1/12	1/13	1/16	1/17	1/18	1/19	1/20	1/23	1/24	1/25	1/26	1/27	1/30	1/31
Create Standardization program to continue the cleaning and keeping things moving forward…including the design of standards posters.	Kelley and Team																						

can start ▭ rliest date on which action

▪ on which action must complete ★ CRITICAL PATH

Process/Actions	Tool	3/2	3/3	3/6	3/7	3/8	3/9	3/10	3/13	3/14	3/15	3/16	3/17	3/20	3/21	3/22	3/23	3/24	3/27	3/28	3/29	3/20	3/31
Spring Cleaning Process	March																						
Continue with next steps of creating visual representation	Kelley																						
Plan for next spring clean	Kelley and Team																						

can start ▭ rliest date on which action

▪ on which action must complete ★ CRITICAL PATH

FIGURE 5.1 (continued)

The brochure included examples of how Shine and Sustain could be accomplished and what things should be considered in each phase (Figure 5.2). A Microsoft PowerPoint presentation (Figure 5.3) was also created for all the volunteer Clean Sweep employees. Questions could be answered during a 1.5 hour training session.

Here are the steps we took to implement the 5S Clean Sweep project:

1. Design and approve all forms, including the blue tag form and equipment removal tag form (Figure 5.4).
2. Design the logo and the posters (Figure 5.5).
3. E-mail all employees and managers, asking for nominations for Clean Sweep volunteers (Figure 5.6).
4. Develop the metrics to be measured in order to analyze the return on investment.
5. Design a crossword puzzle in *STAT* (the online University of Colorado Hospital newsletter) to educate staff about the project (Figure 5.7).
6. Create a Test Your Clean Sweep IQ program in *STAT* (Figure 5.8).
7. Create a calendar of events for each floor/clinic/unit involved in the project (Figure 5.9).

RESULTS AND LESSONS LEARNED

University of Colorado Hospital leadership praised the project for being innovative and producing cost savings for the hospital. After the program was delivered successfully, leadership at the hospital voted to hold two more clean sweeps and one virtual clean sweep (cleaning up computer files, Microsoft Outlook, etc.).

The amount of paper and bulk trash that was thrown away can be seen in Table 5.1. The amount of computer equipment and other nonmedical equipment recycled can be seen in Table 5.2. The amount of biomedical equipment recycled or sold can be seen in Table 5.3. Table 5.4 shows the amount of stationery supply items donated for potential reuse or recycling. Table 5.5 shows the number of employees involved in the Clean Sweep program.

Employees were involved in the day-to-day process by implementing Lean tools that enabled the hospital to increase revenues by reusing supplies, reduce revenues by reducing waste, and increase employee satisfaction scores in value and trust in management.

FIGURE 5.2

Educational brochure.

FIGURE 5.3
PowerPoint training materials.

BLUE TAG			
Category	Equipment Other		
Item Name			
Asset #			
Quantity	Units:	Value	$
Reason- Circle Choice	1. Not needed 2. Defective 3. Use not known 4. Other		
Disposal by:	Department/Unit		
Disposal Method:	1. Discard 2. Return to Vendor 3. Move to Storage Site 4. Other		Disposal Complete (signature)
Today's Date: Blue Tag File #	Posting Date:		Disposal Date:

FIGURE 5.4
Blue tag form.

FIGURE 5.5
Poster and logo.

The 5S Clean Sweep project became the beginning of the Lean initiative for the hospital. Another Lean project took place for the operating room theaters, involving:

- Doctor preference cards: Doctor preference cards were not completed, which led to higher room turnover and inefficient setup of operating room theaters
- Room turnover: Operating room theater turnover was between forty-five and more than sixty minutes, with the national average of twenty-nine minutes
- Sterile processing: Surgical equipment sterile processing was shown as taking too long for surgeries that were back to back
- Presurgery procedures: Patients were being asked the same questions multiple times, which caused patient dissatisfaction

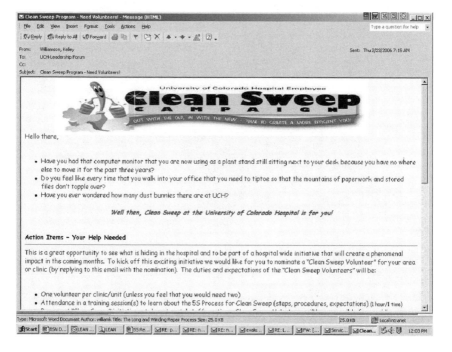

FIGURE 5.6

Volunteer e-mail campaign.

Get Ready For Clean Sweep!
Test Your Knowledge Of UCH's Policies And Procedures

Think of the last time you moved to a new house or apartment. Chances are you took the opportunity to get rid of things you didn't need or want, to avoid moving unnecessary items. That's the philosophy behind our upcoming spring cleaning events—called the 5S Clean Sweep Campaign—starting this month. As we prepare to transition from Ninth Avenue to Fitzsimons, now is the perfect time to examine our work areas and purge or move unnecessary paper documents, extra supplies, broken or unused computers and equipment, and so on. That way, we don't waste time moving clutter, and employees who are moving during the transition can have a fresh, clean start in their new work areas.

Although the move to Fitzsimons inspired our Clean Sweep, the campaign will include everyone—our employees, physicians and volunteers—even if they are not relocating during the transition. The 5S Clean Sweep process we are going to follow is proven to enhance workplace organization, efficiency and productivity. So applying it hospital wide will mean a better environment for our employees, patients and visitors.

Our first hospital-wide 5S Clean Sweep will start later this month. But before we start purging and cleaning, it's important to know the hospital's policies and procedures related to what can be discarded and what needs to be saved. Because you can probably think of a million things you'd rather do than read a bunch of policies and procedures, the Clean Sweep Task Force decided to add some fun by developing a cross word puzzle. All the answers can be found in our Policies and Procedures Web page (look under Quick Links on the iAmaze homepage).

The puzzle is available in the Community Plaza section of iAmaze (under Events). Send your completed puzzle to Kelley Williamson (mail stop A029) by Saturday, April 15, and your name will be entered in a drawing for 10 great prizes. If you have any questions, please contact Kelley, manager of training and development at kelley.williamson@uch.edu or x20856.

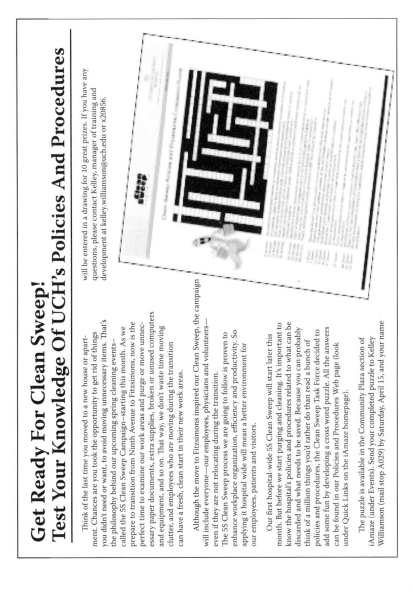

FIGURE 5.7
Crossword puzzle.

Test Your Clean Sweep IQ

By Kelley Williamson, Manager of Training/Development

Are you afraid to have people walk by your office because you know that they will take one look and run the other way? Do you have days when you have to kick things out of the way to just close your door? If you don't have this issue, you probably know others who do.

Fortunately, our upcoming 5S Clean Sweep campaign will help solve these problems across our organization. Before we get started, we want to check everyone's understanding of what life will be like if we work together to make our hospital more efficient. In other words, we want to test your Clean Sweep IQ!

In the photos below, can you guess which office is the Clean Sweep office and which one isn't? The first person to e-mail the correct answer to kelleywilliamson@uch.edu will receive a S5 gift certificate to either Starbucks or Chipoile. (The choice is yours!)

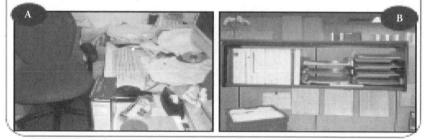

FIGURE 5.8
Test Your Clean Sweep IQ.

Clean Sweep CAMPAIGN

University of Colorado Hospital Employee

OUT WITH THE OLD IN WITH THE NEW – TIME TO CREATE A MORE EFFICIENT 'U'

Spring Cleaning Calendar May 7 - May 25, 2007

The following bins and services will be provided in your area on your designated Spring Cleaning day:

1. **Biomedical Equipment:** For a Clean Sweep of medical equipment call x88361 for pick-up. Please include a signed asset retirement form, manuals, and all accessories including vendor owned PCs for each medical device. Use "Blue Tags".

2. **Infection Services Equipment:** Computer screens, CPUs, keyboards, mice, printers and telephones. Call the Help Desk at x45222 for pick-up. Please include a signed asset retirement form for all UCH owned equipment. Use "Blue Tags".

3. **Paper Waste:** ALL paper waste will be disposed in the large receptacles provided by the Clean Sweep Team. This can include catalogs, books, etc. Paper clips, staples and small fasteners are okay to dispose in the provided containers.

4. **Bulk Waste:** Non-reusable, non-paper items need to be thrown away, noting the following exceptions. DO NOT place furniture, linens, IV poles or biomedical "red bag" waste in the Bulk Waste bin.

5. **Furniture: Absolutely no furniture will be disposed during this Clean Sweep process.** This includes chairs, desks, tables, shelves, cabinets, refrigerator, etc.

6. **Linens:** All soiled linen needs to be processed as normal and thrown in the Soiled Utility Rooms or Linen Chutes.

7. **Hazardous Waste:** Medical waste, chemical waste, pharmaceutical waste, batteries will be processed as normal. Do not put these items in the Bulk trash.

8. **Stationery/Office Supplies:** any unused stationery or unused office supplies (3-ring binders, letterhead, envelopes, pens, highlighters, post-it notes, etc.) need to be kept for future use. All items will need to be dropped off to the Administrative Office Building (AOB) Suite 200.

SUN	MONDAY	TUESDAY	WEDNESDAY	THURSDAY	FRIDAY	SAT
May	7	8	9	10	11	
	8th Floor	8th Floor	8th Floor	8th Floor	8th Floor	
	7th Floor	7th Floor	7th Floor	7th Floor	7th Floor	
	6th Floor	6th Floor	6th Floor	6th Floor	6th Floor	
	5th Floor	5th Floor	5th Floor	5th Floor	5th Floor	
	4th Floor	4th Floor	4th Floor	4th Floor	4th Floor	
	14	15	16	17	18	
	3rd Floor	3rd Floor	3rd Floor	3rd Floor	3rd Floor	
	2nd Floor	2nd Floor	2nd Floor	2nd Floor	2nd Floor	
	1st Floor	1st Floor	1st Floor	1st Floor	1st Floor	
	Basement	Basement	Basement	Basement	Basement	
	AOB	AOB	AOB	AOB	AOB	
	21	22	23	24	25	
	1st Floor CCT	1st Floor CCT	1st Floor CCT	1st Floor CCT	1st Floor CCT	
	2nd Floor CCT	2nd Floor CCT	2nd Floor CCT	2nd Floor CCT	2nd Floor CCT	
	3rd Floor CCT	3rd Floor CCT	3rd Floor CCT	3rd Floor CCT	3rd Floor CCT	
	4th Floor CCT	4th Floor CCT	4th Floor CCT	4th Floor CCT	4th Floor CCT	
	Basement CCT	Basement CCT	Basement CCT	Basement CCT	Basement CCT	

FIGURE 5.9

5S Clean Sweep calendar.

TABLE 5.1

Amount of Paper and Bulk Trash Eliminated

Type	Clean Sweep	Ave. Annual lbs.	Notes
Confidential waste	12,236	55,215	59 100-gallon crates collected at Clean Sweep
Paper recycle waste	7,893	48,650	42 green totes collected at Clean Sweep
Bulk waste	11,920		One open-top construction dumpster collected at Clean Sweep Bulk trash is charged per pull, not per poundage
Total	32,049		

TABLE 5.2

Amount of Computer Equipment and Other Nonmedical Equipment Recycled

Type	No. Recycled	Notes
Computers	15	Recycled
Printers	43	Recycled
Monitors	12	Recycled
Miscellaneous	3	Recycled
Total	73 items	

TABLE 5.3

Amount of Biomedical Equipment Recycled or Sold

Type	No. of Items	Dollars	Notes
Miscellaneous equipment	150–200	$3,350.00	Given to Materials Management department as miscellaneous revenue
Donation	15	$2,500.00	Donated to Madagascar
Total		$5,850.00	

TABLE 5.4

Amount of Stationery Supply Items Donated for Reuse or Recycling

Type	Dollars	Notes
Stationery supplies	$11,000	Miscellaneous supplies that are already being reused
Binders	($1,600.00)	Largest part of the Clean Sweep program for collection
Total	**$11,000.00**	

TABLE 5.5

Number of Employees Involved in Clean Sweep

Type	Number	Notes
Employees	85+	Largest task force formed in the history of the University of Colorado Hospital
Total	**85+**	

6

Applying Lean Thinking to the Outpatient Registration Process

Deborah Miller
Consultant, Fort Wayne, Indiana

PROJECT BACKGROUND

The chief operating officer (COO) of the Dupont Hospital, a midsized, midwestern hospital in the United States, decided to explore Lean in healthcare. Two consulting groups were invited to participate. One group was from a university and the second group comprised local Lean consultants. Two approaches were implemented simultaneously, each without the knowledge of the other.

The university spent a number of weeks analyzing the preoperative and recovery area, using value stream mapping (VSM), and identifying the key operating room (OR) issues. The hospital COO was pleased with the result, which confirmed "gut feelings" and showed that changes needed to be made.

The focus of this case study is the Kaizen event conducted by the Lean consultants.

IMPLEMENTING LEAN

Getting Ready

Discussion began more than two months before the Kaizen event occurred. We decided that management staff needed additional information about Lean in healthcare and what Lean could do for the hospital.

The hospital managers usually attended an optional event, "Teach Me Thursdays," where various topics are presented at a lunch meeting. We decided that four, one-hour sessions would be developed with the Lean consultants and the executive team at the hospital. These meetings were to be highly interactive and provided reinforcement through homework assignments between the sessions. Four Lean consultants rotated delivery of the sessions to provide a variety of expertise and facilitation styles to the hospital staff.

Session One outlined the concepts of Lean Management, Six Sigma, and Lean Six Sigma. These disciplines were introduced and most of the emphasis was placed on Lean Management because of its immediate applicability.

Session Two introduced the concept of "flow" as it applies to work processes and work outcomes. A simulation activity enabled the participants to transfer the concept into their individual frame of reference.

Session Three introduced the concept of the "7 wastes." Participants used affinity diagrams to identify waste in their areas of the hospital.

Session Four provided a discussion of the roles each person would play in the process and, in particular, the role of the Lean champion in successful implementations.

Culture

The culture of the Dupont Hospital is very much focused on the "guest" (patient). Founded on the Disney principles, the hospital is more progressive and creative than most. Its tagline is "Discover the Dupont Difference."

The hospital's mission and values reflect that focus:

> Responding to the healthcare needs of the community, we are committed to excellence in all aspects of care through education, prevention, treatment, and support. We create a five-star experience by exceeding individual expectations for all who enter our door.

The hospital was "built by physicians" to provide better patient care and comfort. Its philosophy is to "treat you more like a privileged guest than a hospital patient." It places considerable emphasis on the quality of care each guest receives.

Choosing the Kaizen Event

In a follow-up meeting with the COO, we determined that we needed a Kaizen event focused on the outpatient registration process. The past three

Gallup surveys showed patient satisfaction in this area to be consistently low, an unacceptable situation for the hospital.

The Kaizen event would take place the following week—only two days' notice! This proved to be an issue later on.

The purpose of the Kaizen event was to "decrease the waiting times our guests experience during the check-in and registration process and to improve the customer satisfaction scores in the outpatient test and treatment areas as identified through the Gallup surveys."

The following method was used: "To dissect and understand the outpatient flow process by mapping, isolating points of waste, initiating immediate recommendations for change, and measuring the impacts of those changes."

The Team

A multidisciplinary team was assembled. The team included representatives from the radiology, laboratory, and surgery registration departments, as well as volunteer services. Other team members included the physician liaison, the team leader for ancillary services, and the food service specialist. More support team members were brought in as the project progressed to address additional concerns and to provide the team with expertise outside the core group.

The specialist in charge of the outpatient registration department was new to the hospital but highly experienced in the registration process. This specialist did not fully understand the new culture and expectations for team action. She was accustomed to handling issues within her area and making all the decisions. This was an uncomfortable situation for her to find herself in: a subject of a Lean project, in a new environment, with others offering suggestions for how "her" area was to improve.

The Kaizen Event

The Lean consultants spent some time observing the patient access process (PAC) prior to the Kaizen event to identify waste and to gain some understanding of the overall process. This information was used during the Kaizen implementation.

Because this was the first Kaizen event for the hospital, the training and planning occurred simultaneously. The Kaizen event was scheduled for a full week, culminating with a presentation and lunch on Friday. Two Lean consultants led the Kaizen event. One of the consultants has considerable experience in leading Kaizen events in manufacturing, while the author (Deborah Miller) has experience in process development for healthcare and in facilitating groups.

Day One—Identifying the Problem

The Kaizen team assembled in a conference room to begin the event. We spent the morning introducing the team and Lean concepts. We incorporated a Lego demonstration of batch versus flow in the morning session.

The Kaizen team then spent time watching the registration process in action and collecting data. It identified the greatest dissatisfactions in the process. Two problem areas emerged: wait times at registration, and wait times at the various service departments (i.e., the radiology department, the laboratory, etc.).

The team decided to address only the wait times at registration in this Kaizen event. The wait times at the service departments would be addressed in future Kaizen events.

The team identified several areas of concern in the outpatient registration process:

- Congestion at point of entry—all visitors to the lobby were directed to the information desk, resulting in long lines during busy periods.
- The PAC team member who was sitting at the information desk did not register guests, so this resource was underutilized.
- The PAC team member or volunteer would escort the guest to the appropriate registration waiting area (laboratory or radiology), resulting in multiple hand-offs.
- If a guest presented without orders or appointment, the guest was routinely given the phone to speak with the appropriate service area and asked personal health information (PHI) questions. There was no safeguarding of information while at the information desk.

Three types of guests were identified:

1. Scheduled and preregistered
2. Scheduled and not preregistered
3. Not scheduled and not preregistered

Pre-Registered Guest

1. Stop at info desk
2. Talk to registration person at desk (or visitor rep or volunteer)
3. Registrar records name, arrival time, appointment time
4. Guest gets out insurance card, photo ID
5. Guest is escorted back to waiting lobby
6. Registrar goes into work room and pulls order
7. Order put into jacket with ID and put into wall holder
8. Guest goes in PAC booth
9. PAC has paperwork printed out—verifies DOB, name
10. Guest signs consents, scans patient copy and insurance info
    a. Consent to Treat
    b. Protected Healthcare Info (PHI)
    c. HIPAA Brochure
    d. If medicare, ABN & Medicare Rights
11. Review Benefits and Collect Co-Pay
12. Place Armband
13. Guest back to waiting room

FIGURE 6.1
Lists of process steps at registration.

Day Two—Collecting the Data

To demonstrate the registration process for the team, we simulated a worst-case scenario for a guest registration. "Joan Taylor," a nonscheduled, non-preregistered guest, presented at the information desk. The time to complete the registration process from front desk to the radiology room was thirty-five minutes. The number of "true" guests waiting registration at that time was considered very low.

The team then spent the remainder of the day collecting data and identifying the steps that each guest must go through to be registered. The resulting process steps were listed, as shown in Figure 6.1.

Days Three and Four—Implementing Changes

The time for action arrived. We decided that a number of steps should be implemented to get guests registered quickly. A preregistered guest kiosk

Non-Registered Guest (Order in Hand)

1. Repeat steps 1–6 of Pre-Reg. Guest
2. Guest goes into registration booth
3. SSN search to determine prior visits in Dupont
4. Guest name recorded and searches enterprise-wide for previous visits and information
5. PAC enters name, DOB, gender, race, home address, mailing address, city, state, zip, phone number, "Can we leave a message?", SSN, place of employment, F/T, P/T, address, phone number, occupation

Approval to treat if a child

Quick Registration Fields:
Relation 1 (1st emergency contact)—Name
If spouse, address, contact
If insurance carrier, inst. Owner Name, SSN
Employment of Relative 1
Relative 2 (optional) Name and phone # only

Medical Page—Location (OPT, ins), priority level, walk-in/emg/critical, date & time, diagnosis, outpatient approval (if applicable)

COW
Insurance section—insurance info and LOBE1
Notes for PHI, copies of mat, ABM percent & remittances

6. PAC Continued
   a. Current Codes
   b. Physician's Page—admitting, attending, PCP, ER
   c. Print screen—code in jacket for forms
   d. Custom deisgned fields
   e. System-assigned medical report number and patient number

7. Continue back to Pre-Reg Gust steps 10–13

FIGURE 6.1 (continued).

is in the planning and testing stages and, once online, it will alleviate the wait time for preregistered guests. The kiosk will help with only one type of guest.

We decided to move the PAC resource from the information desk and set up an express check-in desk to move preregistered guests through the

FIGURE 6.1 (continued).

system more quickly. A volunteer or other staff member would be present at the express check-in desk to escort guests who would need to complete the full registration process. The PAC team member would remain at the desk at all times and would be available to assist with the kiosk process as needed.

The team knew of a desk in storage and worked with the IT resource and facilities manager to get the desk set up and functional by Thursday morning.

The volunteers and PAC team members were informed of the changes and implemented them to test effectiveness.

Preregistered guests could now sign consents, receive their arm band, and have their insurance and ID cards scanned at the express check-in desk. The guests would then be escorted directly to the service queue instead of the registration queue. The paperwork for the guest was immediately available to the service area.

We had determined that entering insurance information while the guest was in the registration area was a non-value-added step. During busy periods, insurance information could be entered outside the registration booth by a "floater." This person would also be available to assist PACs with copying, running charts, and so forth. This reduces the number of times a PAC has to leave the guest alone in the booth. A computer on wheels (COW) was borrowed and added to the workroom between registration areas to facilitate the insurance entry. A permanent computer was ordered to replace the borrowed equipment.

FIGURE 6.1 (continued).

We started a 5S of the registration hub area. We determined, due to staffing pressures, that the PAC staff would complete additional work at a later date. During the first phase of the 5S, we determined that some of the copy equipment would be relocated to an area outside the registration hub; equipment was moved and the COW was added.

FIGURE 6.1 (continued).

The PAC staff had scanning equipment on their desks, but this equipment was not functional most of the time. IT was brought in to address the open issues immediately and the equipment use was monitored during the Kaizen event. It was also suggested that desk printers be ordered for each of the registration areas. The printers are deemed a special order, due to the requirement for printing armbands, stickers, and paperwork. The printers were added to the future requirements list. These printers will further reduce the time PACs must leave the guest in the registration area.

A quick registration screen was identified in the registration software as being available and underused by the registration staff. This quick registration screen can be used for noninvasive procedures, for example, radiology without contrast. The use of this screen can save the registrars approximately two minutes for each guest by not having to enter additional contact information.

We also determined that "special procedures" guests should be preregistered by the surgical scheduling department instead of the registration team, because these guests require a nurse to perform a history and physical (H&P) prior to the procedure. This means such guests can arrive closer to their actual procedure time and be placed in the queue immediately. It reduces the guest wait time by up to two hours.

Then we discovered that hospital employees, referring physicians, and guests were unaware that they could preregister via the Internet. The Kaizen team met with the marketing representative to identify changes to the online preregistration process. In addition, updated preregistration notification cards and placards were also ordered to increase awareness. An e-mail was sent to all hospital employees to increase their awareness of the process. As it happened, Dr. Eastlund, vice president for physician liaison and the Dupont Resource Center, used the online registration for a procedure he required during the week of the Kaizen event. By using the online registration process, he reported that it took ten minutes, from the time he reached the lobby to the time he was discharged, to have a blood draw.

The central scheduling department will begin to request more insurance data during the scheduling process. It is believed that the physician offices have the information when they call, and capturing the information at that time will help to reduce the calls that preregistration requires. Central Scheduling also receives faxed insurance information that is currently not used for preregistration. These faxed forms will be filed and made available for the preregistration process. Central Scheduling will also become an advocate for the online preregistration process with office schedulers and guests.

By Thursday afternoon, the Kaizen team was ready to finalize the documentation and draft the final Microsoft PowerPoint presentation for the executive team and managers.

Day Five—Recommendations

The Kaizen team spent part of the morning collecting data on the changes made on Wednesday and Thursday. The final procedure change documentation and PowerPoint presentation were completed.

The Kaizen team identified the following items for follow-up and assigned responsibilities and deadlines for completion. The list of items included:

- Marketing support (in process)
- Physician office education (in process)
- Team training—new hires, new roles, new processes
- Special procedures guests for preregistration move to Surgery Scheduling
- Portal access for data collection to online preregistration
- Complete 5S for central hub for PAC
- COW replaced by permanent PC in hub
- Signage for express check-in desk and kiosk
- Periodic follow-up to sustain changes

After a celebration lunch, the Kaizen team made the final presentation to the executive team and managers.

RESULTS AND LESSONS LEARNED

In the weeks following the Kaizen event, the Lean consultants met once again with the COO of the hospital to see how the event affected the process.

The team had tweaked the process. An information desk was placed closer to the door with a volunteer staff person who could then direct people to the appropriate areas. This reduced the queues at the preregistration desk.

The COO had implemented a weekly scorecard for the PAC team. As a result of the changes in the processes, 87 to 95 percent of patients were now preregistered. Weekly Gallup survey scores had risen to acceptable levels.

An additional benefit to the organization was that there was a commitment to use the Lean methodologies to pull together to fix problems. Members of the team were sharing the knowledge they received from the Kaizen event with others and beginning to identify and improve additional areas within the hospital.

The Kaizen team took a single line process that had inherent delays and batching, that averaged thirty minutes, and had no options for different types of guests (as shown in Figure 6.2).

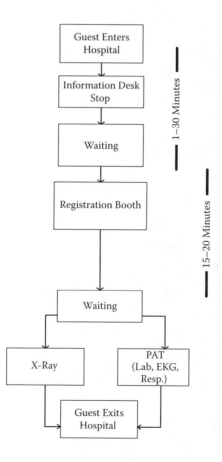

FIGURE 6.2
The original single-line process.

Note that the time to complete the registration process was between sixteen and fifty minutes. Long waits were not unusual.

The future state became a multiline process that allows for the sorting of guests by type, thus reducing the wait time for two of the three guest types (as shown in Figure 6.3).

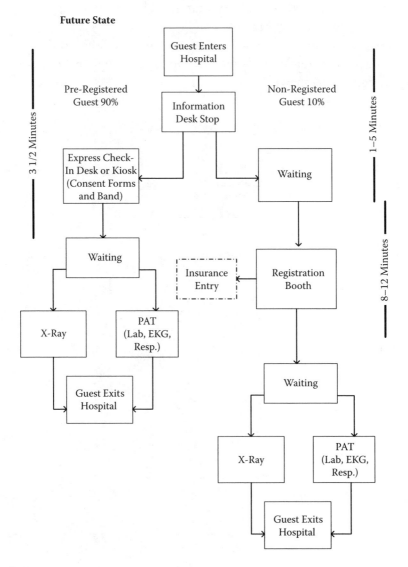

FIGURE 6.3
The new multiline process.

The communication for this project was not as thorough as it could have been. The two-day start following the decision to take action resulted in communication challenges as the project progressed.

Even though we had spent time upfront educating the managers, the optional nature of the Teach Me Thursdays resulted in key managers not being fully prepared or understanding the nature of the process.

It takes time to adjust to the culture of the organization. For new managers, it could feel overwhelming to take on a new position and a new culture and then a Lean project in their area, when they are just getting a handle on the job as well. This could prove a very threatening situation to a new manager. Additional coaching for the managers would have been helpful.

Although it is important to move quickly once a decision to implement Lean in an organization is made, care must be taken to ensure that relevant stakeholders have a full understanding of the process before the project begins.

Change is always unsettling, even when all the parties involved are committed to the outcome. Taking the time to brief the stakeholders ensures cooperation and reduces the stress during and immediately following the improvement event.

This hospital has a great culture. Staff members are willing to work together to ensure their guests receive the best quality care and service possible. The participants embraced the concepts of Lean and are spreading the message throughout the hospital. The COO considered the project a success and will be implementing additional projects in the future.

7

Establishing a Standardized and Efficient Client Laboratory Supplies Process

Christian Buchsteiner
Oregon Medical Laboratories, Springfield, Oregon

PROJECT BACKGROUND

In this chapter I share one of my improvement case studies to give you a good overview on how successful and powerful Lean can be. It has certainly helped reduce wastes and increase value and reliability of services in the laboratory processes at Oregon Medical Laboratories. It also decreased the frustration and facilitated the development of mutual trust and respect that are necessary to make you and your organization a winning team.

Company Profile

Oregon Medical Laboratories (OML) is one of the largest independent not-for-profit medical and occupational testing laboratories in the Pacific Northwest. Owned by PeaceHealth and headquartered in Springfield, Oregon, with laboratory and collection sites throughout the region, OML offers more than 1,000 different medical diagnostic tests, clinical laboratory consultation, and drug testing.

OML serves more than 5,000 Northwest physicians' offices, hospitals, nursing homes, clinics, and businesses. In 2007, the company performed more than seven million tests. The challenges are to manage a very diverse lab environment, from supporting a 450-bed inpatient hospital environment to servicing a very large and growing outreach community within the State of Oregon and beyond.

The OML main laboratory operations had previously been located near downtown Eugene, where it still maintains a laboratory dedicated to providing services for Sacred Heart Medical Center. The previous location enabled OML to provide more than 45 percent of the state's reference laboratory services. However, the new open, single-floor laboratory space allows for the addition of new automated technologies that will ultimately provide patients with faster test results and enhance the hospital's services.

The Hospital Move

The move to the new location at River Bend required a strategy for managing growth, opportunities, and overall change. The leadership team appreciated that this change required focus, so it decided to use Lean Thinking.

Soon after the move, several employees (led by OML executive leadership and supported by outside resources) were trained in Lean Thinking and in applying Lean tools, including Six Sigma. A pilot project was identified in the preanalytical specimen management department to enhance turnaround time, accuracy, and throughput.

I already had extensive experience in Six Sigma and Kaizen and had the opportunity to further enhance my skills by being trained and certified as a Lean Healthcare Green Belt by the Leading Edge Group.

IMPLEMENTING LEAN

The Problem

OML provides supplies for specimen collection and results management. This process covers all activities from the time the supply request is placed by the client until the supplies are delivered. It is a cross-functional process and, over time, it has become more complex. Additional complexity is added by ensuring compliance with regulatory affairs. Frequent supply audits per client to verify supply consumption with testing activities are required by the Center for Medicare/Medicaid and the Stark II law and Anti-Kickback statutes, and records of such also need to be available.

In the past, the entire process was overseen by OML. Process ownership and customized systems helped to ensure that OML complied with the regulations and met clients' needs. The materials management function was centralized with the PeaceHealth materials management department, and a vendor relationship was established. As a result, new technology was introduced so people could order supplies through an outdated electronic hospital inventory management system. This made it more difficult for staff to order and track requests or communicate issues as they arose, adding time and bureaucracy to the process.

Over a fifteen-month period, multiple attempts at solving this problem consistently failed. While at times it seemed on the surface that the situation had improved, the entire process still lacked the required process stability, consistency, and standardization. Client complaints, long and excessive turn around time (TAT), lost supplies, duplicate supplies, wrong units, excessive supplies per client, inability to ensure compliance, and so on were common occurrences.

Clients were unhappy, the reputation of OML as a quality laboratory was in jeopardy, and employees on both sides of the process were frustrated. OML leadership recognized that the client laboratory supplies management process needed some immediate attention, as it was having a direct impact on core values and business.

The Lean Journey

In the first meeting with the oversight team (which comprised cross-functional process owners and OML leadership), we established the project scope, goals, and expectations. We discussed all performance issues and concerns regarding the OML supply chain—both internal and external. It was soon apparent that *both* needed attention, so it seemed logical to address both at the same time. We decided to use a Lean approach known as "choosing the right service family."

Choosing the Right Service Family

It was clear that the core service was the supply order. However, OML uses multiple supply chains and streams, with different steps and processes. To capture these differences, we had to outline all process steps, the variations, and the data on frequency and volume. We used a simple grid and collected preliminary data to determine which streams were used most. This provided us with a high-level overview of the OML supply chain and enabled us to prioritize our approaches.

What's Going Wrong?

In this phase, it was important to provide a voice to all participants and capture the issues. We used brainstorming techniques to identify the key issues (see Table 7.1 on the opposite page).

Equipped with this summary, the oversight team was able to generate the scope for the process improvement team.

Project Scope

The Lean design team had to establish a cross-functional, standardized, simple, and effective process to manage client supply orders from the time the request is placed until the supplies are delivered. It needed to:

- Ensure preparation and delivery of the right (type and number) supplies—on time and at the right time (JIT) in a professional and efficient manner
- Help to generate standard operating procedures (SOPs) and training manuals for all departments involved
- Put in place a process to review and approve supplies that can be ordered by clients
- Support testing methodologies
- Develop a process to communicate (specifically to clients and client services) when supplies and/or vendors are discontinued and/or changed
- Establish an audit and monitoring system to observe consumption of supplies and to test order patterns
- Ensure an easy ordering process, primarily for OML clients but also for internal order placement

Process Performance Baseline

The problems with current performance were as follows:

- Client complaints (percent of all supply orders placed, monitored since 09/2006) = 1.26 percent or 3.74 Sigma.

TABLE 7.1

An Outline of the Key Problems and Desired Outcomes

	Problem Statement	**Desired Outcomes and Benefits**
Patient care	The lack of supplies or the ability to generate results at the client offices is jeopardizing or delaying the patient's diagnosis and/or treatment.	• Improved patient care
Client retention	Clients are dissatisfied with OML and its ability to manage the supply chain. Clients may leave OML. This not only means the loss of business, but also the loss of reputation and is affecting the OML strategy for growth.	• Improved client satisfaction • Enhanced growth
Compliance	Supply audit and monitoring are not happening on a consistent basis as required by regulatory agencies.	• Regulatory compliance • Enhanced transparency
Frustration	Ongoing unresolved issues are adding to the frustrations of all involved.	• Enhanced teamwork and communication • Elimination of existing cross-functional boundaries
Cost	There is no supply monitoring or supply budget oversight/ownership.	• Opportunity of cost savings in excess of $100,000 annually
Testing excellence	Substituting supplies when vendors discontinue and/or change existing supplies requires communication to the OML testing criteria and specification. Need to avoid specimen recollects and affecting testing accuracy. No formal approval, communication, and documentation process is in place.	• Supply review and approval process to respond to changes and communicate these in an effective manner • Potential supply standardization, streamlining of internal operations, and standardization of existing and future processes
Process documentation	Process procedures and manuals are not available, resulting in the lack of a foundation for successful cross-functional operation.	• All required process documentation, including plans and competency assessments • Enhanced process accountability, transparency, and process ownership

- TAT was exceeding the client expectation of twenty-four hours from the time the supply order is placed to delivery—this was particularly an issue with clients in Portland.
- Costs of supplies were not monitored.
- No audits were performed and corrective actions were not taken.
- No formal supplies approval process was in place.
- SOPs, training, and competency assessment were not in place.

Success Criteria

The success criteria were as follows:

- Number of complaints placed by clients to client services and sales are reduced by 50 percent from baseline after completion of project.
- Supply order TAT from order placement to delivery does not to exceed forty-eight hours.
- TAT on 90 percent of supply orders does not to exceed twenty-four hours.
- 75 percent of all OML clients are audited in 2007—documentation and corrective action plans are in place.

The Team

After the scope was identified, we formed a cross-functional team with participants from all departments. It consisted of primarily front-line staff with management and executive oversight, led by the author. And so the journey began …

Value Definition

We challenged all team members to see the service from the clients' perspective. This would help them to establish the clients' needs and to ascertain what would add value to the operation. The OML marketing and sales team interviewed and surveyed clients to better understand their needs and expectations.

Voice of Customer (VOC) = Professional Packaging × Speedy Delivery × Easy Ordering × Complete Delivery

Throughout the project, the team was very creative in identifying other opportunities for improving this process. It was striving to create an exceptional supply chain, one that would add more value to the client operation and would also set us apart from other laboratory providers.

Process Flow

Because the team comprised members from all the involved departments, it was important for us to "walk the existing process." This would ensure that everybody was on the same page, and understood the activities, processes, tools, and systems involved. It provided a sense of camaraderie, breaking down barriers from the onset. It also helped everybody understand what actually happens from the time supplies are requested by the client until they are ready to be delivered. As a result of the process walks, we generated simple flowcharts for all processes, including exception handling as required.

The Current State VSM

Using the value stream mapping (VSM) tool enabled the entire organization to understand its current cross-functional process. Furthermore, it helped us to quantify the value-added and non-value-added steps.

We generated a simple template for VSM, using Microsoft Excel. Outlining and establishing the VSM was very easy. What was more challenging was collecting the required data and calculating value-added and non-value-added times.

The team brainstormed ideas on how to collect the required data and measure the entire process. Unfortunately, no system data was available. Therefore, we generated a manual cross-functional measurement plan. This plan included capturing how the supply orders were submitted and also the client's geographical location. Over a period of two weeks, the times for each supply order were recorded.

After we completed the data collection, we analyzed the data and calculated the value-added and non-value-added times. The data was then transferred to the current state VSM (see Figure 7.1 on the following page).

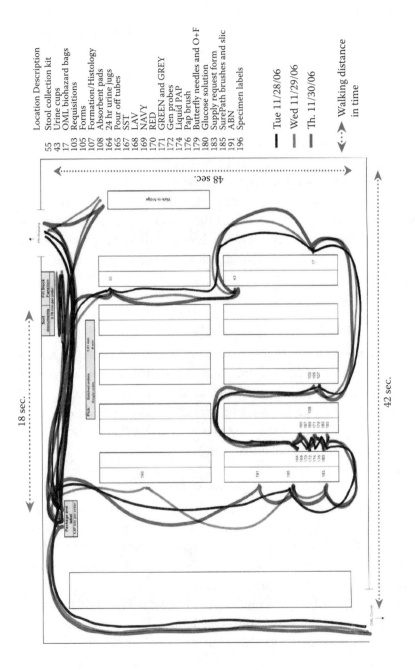

Location	Description
55	Stool collection kit
43	Urine cups
17	OML biohazard bags
103	Requisitions
105	Forms
107	Formation/Histology
108	Absorbent pads
164	24 hr urine jugs
165	Pour off tubes
167	SST
168	LAV
169	NAVY
170	RED
171	GREEN and GREY
172	Gen probes
174	Liquid PAP
176	Pap brush
179	Butterfly needles and O+F
180	Glucose solution
183	Supply request form
185	SurePath brushes and slic
191	ABN
196	Specimen labels

—— Tue 11/28/06
—— Wed 11/29/06
—— Th. 11/30/06

‹···› Walking distance in time

FIGURE 7.1
Current state VSM.

TABLE 7.2

Current State Process Performance

Process Speed	Baseline	Process Accuracy	Baseline
Total average process lead time	22.13 hr	Client satisfaction	97.41% = 3.44 Sigma
Average NVA (opportunity time)	16.67 hr	Inventory shortage	95.20% = 3.16 Sigma
Average VA	5.47 hr	Supply order entry performance	95.04% = 3.15 Sigma
Orders delivered within 24 hr	55.30%		
Orders delivered within 48 hr	98.80%		
Orders exceeding 48 hr	1.20%		

Data Summary

Table 7.2 is a summary of the current state process performance. It was established by VSM and by identifying and measuring key process performance measures.

We also focused on establishing key performance measures and started to monitor these on an ongoing basis. We used graphs to display the performance measures. In some cases, we used Pareto charts to identify key issues. These were very helpful in developing action plans to resolve and improve performance.

Client services and our sales team recorded any client complaints regarding the supply process (Figure 7.2).

Whenever there was a supply shortage, the inventory management system generated a shortage report. This report was faxed to client services

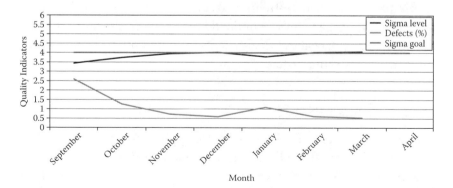

FIGURE 7.2
Complaints from clients about the supply process.

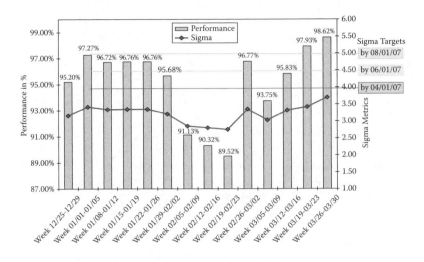

FIGURE 7.3
Shortage report.

and then the client was called. All these reports were logged and a Pareto chart generated. This chart showed items with a high shortage frequency and the data was used to identify root causes and solutions (see Figure 7.3 above and Figure 7.4 on the opposite page).

We also had to capture the supply order entry performance, because a failure in this step resulted in the client getting the wrong item or the wrong quantity. About 32.9 percent of the orders are called in by the client. The team acknowledged that these orders were placed the fastest, but were also the most error prone because of transcription errors.

This process required attention (see Figure 7.5 and Figure 7.6 on page 98). One of the team's recommendations was to eliminate the call-in option and replace it by asking clients to submit orders by fax or offer a web-based ordering system.

The Future State VSM

The next step was to teach the team how to apply Lean Thinking. The current state VSM and the collected data were analyzed with the objectives of transforming the process, eliminating wastes, and improving accuracy and speed. We generated a future state VSM, outlining the proposals to improve the process.

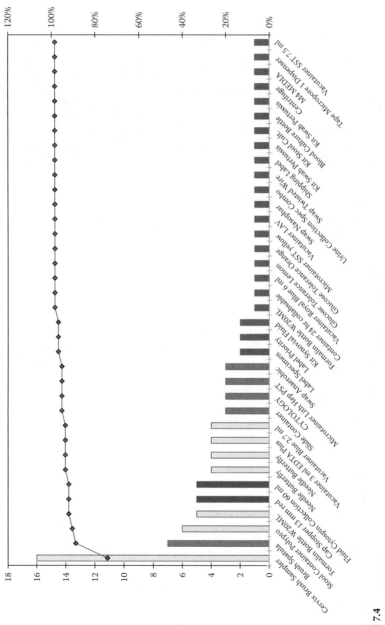

FIGURE 7.4

Pareto chart of shortages per supply item for period from December 26, 2006 through March 31, 2007.

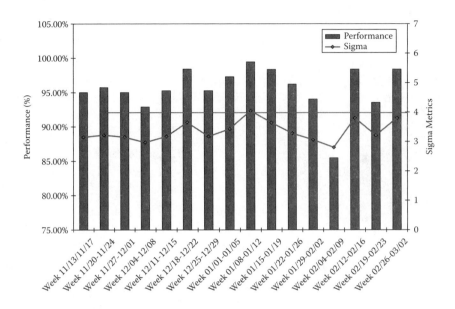

FIGURE 7.5
Supply order entry performance.

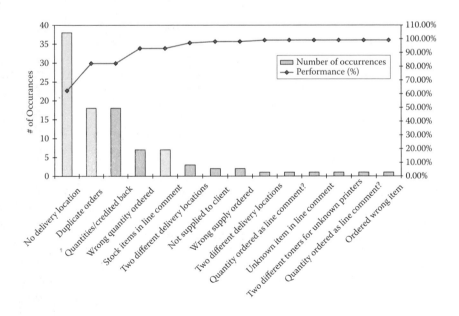

FIGURE 7.6
Pareto chart of supply order entry performance.

Each step in the process was identified with a number. (Numbers 3 to 11 are the Kaizen opportunities.)

1. Design/establish/train: The team identified these items as crucial. Although there are some processes in place, these depend on someone who has been in this position for a long period of time. The existing processes lack the required procedures and standardization.
2. Process performance criteria: During the measurement phase, the team identified a number of key process measurements. These were measured on an ongoing basis. The data was graphed as a Pareto chart. This helped the team to actively address the issues by identifying the root causes. A good example was the supply inventory performance, where within two one-hour meetings the performance was improved by almost 75 percent.
3. Improve supply order placement: There were many variables in the process. Standardization and cross-training will ensure accurate and timely supply order placement.
4. Standardized packaging: As voiced by our sales team, some of our clients felt that the packaging and labeling of supplies were insufficient.
5. Ensure supply tracking and consumption control: Laboratories are required to ensure that only supplies for specimen collection and results managing are provided. This required us to monitor and track usage.
6. Supply delivery (OML versus other): The courier's primary focus was to pick up and drop off specimens. Adding supply delivery may be a cost-effective solution, but could actually negatively affect the TAT on all other specimens.
7. Improve warehouse preparation and pick process:

   NVA (non-value-added) time from order placement to pick start = 490 min

   The pick process itself took about an average of 75 minutes. Applying 5S and utilizing existing spaghetti maps may offer a great opportunity to streamline this process—additional warehouse-specific VSM may be needed.
8. Eliminate call-in supply orders: About 33 percent of orders were called in by clients. These were prone to transcription errors and also

had an impact on the ability of client services to respond to other clients' questions.

9. Reduce NVA times for form submission by OML courier: About 42 percent of all supply OML couriers brought in orders. The NVA time before the order was entered into the inventory management system was an average of 776 minutes, compared to 8 minutes when called in or 44 minutes when faxed.

Replace 8 and 9 by offering an online supply order capability through the OML web site.

10. Improve NVA time before delivery for all clients:

NVA time = average of 109 min

11. Portland supply process:

Portland NVA time before delivery = average of 605 min

The team felt that one of the options to improve this process might be to bring the supplies closer to our clients in Portland, by having in-line client supply inventory or a "supermarket" at our Portland lab and then managing the supply order process from this location.

Value Stream Plan

After we completed the future state VSM, we generated the opportunity log (see Figure 7.7 on the opposite page). The assignment for the project team members was to share and communicate the future state VSM and opportunity log with their co-workers and to ask for feedback and input. Additional items were added to the list as required.

The team then reviewed and ranked each item on the list and established a working priority. The log includes the team or individuals responsible for the task (Who?), expected completion date (When?), and progress report (% complete).

Ranking key:			
VOC	Low = 1	Medium = 3	High = 9
Ease of implementation	Difficult = 1	Medium = 3	Easy = 9
Impact on internal operations	Low = 1	Medium = 3	High = 9

#	Problem/Issue	Ideas/Opportunities	Total Rank	Who?	By When?	Kind of Meeting Scheduled	% Complete			
							25%	50%	75%	100%
	"Fill and Kill" – supply shortage report handling	Establish a process			**3/7/2007**	X				
1	Stock items versus non-stock items	**Can we reduce the number of non-stock client supplies items in our system?**	**31**	Kelly, Shanna, Dave, Walker	3/31/2007					
	Restricted supplies				3/7/2007					
	Inventory levels/shortages	**How can we eliminate shortages?**			Ongoing	X				
2	Process ownership	Can we define a process owner?	**29**	Greg Clark and Larry Morrison	**4/1/2007**	X				
		Communication/ Continuous Improvement/Leadership								

FIGURE 7.7
Opportunity log.

#	Problem/Issue	Ideas/Opportunities	Total Rank	Who?	By When?	Kind of Meeting Scheduled	% Complete			
							25%	50%	75%	100%
	Supply Form Update	Update and modify Supply order form								
	Client Supplies form not up to date; unit and names don't match ESI									
	Too many items on the form?									
3	Quality of faxed form – too dark, difficult to read	**Can we enlarge the fonts sizes on the form?**	29	Sherry	3/31/2007	X				
	Eliminated Supply from Stock item – outdated as soon as printed									
	Units for Formalin bottles?									
	Standardized printed to clients? Printer as stock item, and so the toner?									
4	Supply approval process and substitute supply order process	Establish a process	28	Sherry	**3/15/2007**	X				
5	Time it takes from delivery by courier to client services data entry in ESI too long – average 776 min.	Can we eliminate this submission format? And/or streamline existing process?	28	Project Team	**3/7/2007**	X				

							X			
	Client supply order placement	Can we designate a core group of individuals within CS to enter supply orders at a certain time of the day?		Kelly	3/7/2007	X				
	ESI features	**Does CS know about all available features?**		Nathan/Andrea	**3/7/2007**	X				
6	ESI training	Update ESI SOP	25	Nathan/Andrea	**3/7/2007**	X				
	Enhance/improve order placement performance	**Monitor and improve**		Kelly, Andrea and Nathan	**3/7/2007**	X				
	Non-stock items ordering	**What is the existing process for ordering non-stock items?**		Andrea, Kelly, Chris	**3/7/2007**	X				
7	Supply returns	Can we reduce the number of supply returns?	24	Andrea, Nathan	**Ongoing**					

FIGURE 7.7 (continued)
Opportunity log.

#	Problem/Issue	Ideas/Opportunities	Total Rank	Who?	By When?	Kind of Meeting Scheduled	% Complete			
							25%	50%	75%	100%
8	Client set up in ESI – or how does Client information (Complete name and address) print on documents generated out of ESI	Review and analyze client setup process in ESI. Can addresses be added to ESI and if not can we review supply ordering process-adding client address as a line item?	24	Kelly, Dave, Andrea, and Andrea B.	3/31/2007	X				
	Client address not on delivery form			Project Team/ Vivian/ Dave	3/31/2007	X				
	Not all clients are set up in ESI				3/31/2007	X				
	Supply inventory									
9	Client supplies Management (ordering) software		24	Project Team/ Vivian/ Dave	5/1/2007					
	No supply tracking and consumption control	**How do we accomplish supply tracking – supplies out vs. tests in per client?**								
10	Express Order process	Establish a process	23	Diann, Kelly, Walker	2/23/2007	X				
11	Although called in supply orders are processed the fastest, they pose a great risk of transcription error (item and units)	Can we eliminate this process and standardize the way clients submit supply order requests?	20	Project Team	3/15/2007					

#						
12	Inconsistent packaging and labeling	Standardize boxes, include OML logo and review with Sales	**19**	Chris, Sherry, Andrea B., Marketing	**3/7/2007**	X
	Packaging and labeling SOP				3/7/2007	X
	Client info. on packing slip				3/7/2007	X
13	Process Standardization				?	
	Client?	**Review/establish SOP current state**			?	
	Client Services	**Review/establish SOP current state**	**19**	Everybody	?	
	PHOR MM	**Review/establish SOP current state**			?	
	Transportation	**Review/establish SOP current state**			?	
	Non-stock item process	**What is it?**			?	
14	Client supplies operational consolidation	Can we have one person manage these processes, stock and all non-stock items, from ordering through picking and delivering?	**16**	Project Team/Planning team	**?**	

FIGURE 7.7 (continued)
Opportunity log.

#	Problem/Issue	Ideas/Opportunities	Total Rank	Who?	By When?	Kind of Meeting Scheduled	% Complete			
							25%	50%	75%	100%
15	Supply delivery – OML versus PH Material Management	What is the best way to ensure efficient and timely supply delivery?	**15**	Diann, Walker, Shanna Sherry (Greg and Larry)	?					
	Supply transport/delivery				5/1/2007					
16	Portland	**Can we shorten this time? Currently average of 720 min NVA time – in-line client supplies inventory at our Portland Lab**	13	Kathy, Diann, Mona	5/1/2007					

						X				
17	Warehouse prep and pick process	Can this process be improved?		Nathan, Walker, Dave	3/31/2007	X				
	Walking distance for a supply pick	**Review Spaghetti Map and inventory locations**		Nathan, Walker, Dave	3/31/2007	X				
	Fill Stock Function	**Can we reduce the time between ESI order placement and when the Fill Stock function is performed? Currently average of 490 min. NVA time**	7	Nathan, Walker, Dave	3/31/2007	X				
	ESI doesn't collate documents after fill stock function is performed	**Review ESI capabilities— Example: Can ESI collate documents?**		Nathan, Walker, Dave	3/31/2007	X				
18	Supply replenishment based on consumption patterns	Can we change our process to take over inventory management for (defined) clients and replenish supplies by establishing a KANBAN system? Moving from a push system to a pull system based on consumption.	5	Everybody	?					

FIGURE 7.7 (continued)
Opportunity log.

Kaizen Efforts—A3 Process

The team used the A3 process to facilitate Kaizen events. In some cases, it was able within two hours to take the existing process apart, define a target condition, and establish a testing and implementation plan. This process has proved very efficient and successful, because it is an interactive way to engage each team member. Visualizing and drawing the existing and the future condition helped tremendously. These drawings complemented the data and ideas very well (see Figure 7.8 on the opposite page).

> **Example:** Why does it take 776 min from the time a supply order is generated until it is entered when the form is delivered by the courier department?

During this two-hour event, the team identified a number of potential improvement opportunities. The team focused on the easiest one at this stage: "How can hand-offs be reduced?" The team identified that having a fax machine next to the dispatch desk in the courier department would eliminate all OML internal hand-offs and the travel time for the form. The team generated an implementation plan, including testing of the new process. This new process was rolled out to the team within one week and re-measuring happened shortly thereafter.

RESULTS AND LESSONS LEARNED

Result

With the new process, the NVA of 776 minutes was reduced to 211 minutes for this specific process. This resulted in a 73 percent improvement and reduced the overall process NVA time by 3.89 hours!

Although the team made some great improvements in this specific process, it is still trying to eliminate this entire step and provide a process and system where the form is either faxed by the client's office to client services or submitted by using a web-based program for supply ordering.

The Success

One of the biggest successes in the initial phase was the review of the current state VSM and the process performance data. It allowed everybody to

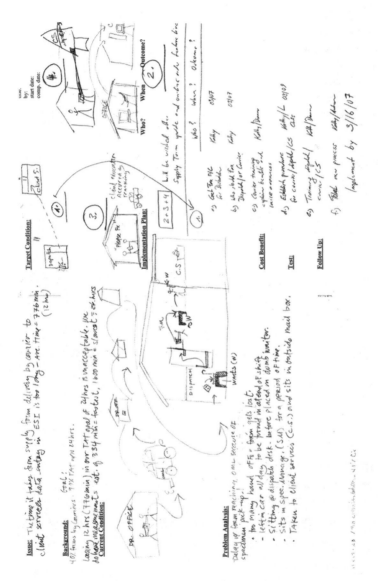

FIGURE 7.8

Visualization of implementation plan.

TABLE 7.3

Improvements in Process Speed

Process Speed	Baseline	Three-Month Progress	Improvement (%)
Total average process lead time	22.13 hr	18.25 hr	16.40%
Average NVA (opportunity time)	16.67 hr	12.78 hr	23.34%
Average VA	5.47 hr	5.47 hr	0%
Orders delivered within 24 hr	55.30%	91.8%	39.76%
Orders delivered within 48 hr	98.80%	100%	1.20%
Orders exceeding 48 hr	1.20%	0%	1.20%

TABLE 7.4

Improvements in Process Accuracy

Process Accuracy	Baseline	Three-Month Progress	Improvement (%)
Client satisfaction	97.41% = 3.44 Sigma	99.48% = 4.06 Sigma	15.27%
Inventory shortage	95.20% = 3.16 Sigma	98.62% = 3.70 Sigma	17.09%
Supply order entry performance	95.04% = 3.15 Sigma	98.39% = 3.80 Sigma	20.63%

see and understand the process and its performance—it provided a common language, and reached out to everybody involved, regardless of organizational structures and divisions.

It gave the team the necessary bearings. At the beginning, everybody felt in foreign territory, but then it was as if someone dropped a map with a red dot displaying "You are here." The current state VSM and the data served as a great visualization of the process. It demonstrated the value of VSM and the importance of data.

A three-month progress report demonstrated measurable successes (Table 7.3 and Table 7.4). Although these gains are very impressive, ongoing efforts are planned to further improve and maintain this process.

Lessons Learned

Using Lean

These improvement efforts demonstrate how Lean Thinking methods can be used in a systematic and very successful manner. The results were very positive. With any project, it is important to reflect on the "base camp" review to identify what worked well and what were some of the obstacles. This reflective step is very important before you go forward. It provides a great opportunity to learn and to adjust the course and future approaches accordingly.

The leadership team was very committed to and supportive of Lean methods. After the first rounds of reviewing the current state VSM and performance data, it realized that the process was actually working much better than previously assumed. As a result, the project was no longer treated as a priority, which slowed execution of important recommendations and action items.

It is important that you follow through, commit, and dedicate. Improvement is a constant effort and not limited to the duration of a project. If it's obvious that you have an opportunity to improve, do it and don't delay.

Selecting the Team

The cross-functional improvement team accomplished a lot, considering it was one of its first Lean projects. For any project, it is extremely important to select the "right" team members. Look for engaged, positive, well-respected individuals, with the skills and attitude to make things better, regardless of existing boundaries, procedures, or processes.

Selecting team members involves more than just selecting the most experienced person. You have to find the right person, with the heart and soul to make things better. Your 100 percent support for this team is required—so check in frequently.

Using Project Management Tools

One of the requests from the leadership team was to use project management tools to support Lean efforts. Although success criteria were required, they are a contradiction to Lean Thinking and may be a hindrance in the continuous improvement process. When the established success criteria were met, the team reacted to this with a sense of completion.

Make a conscious decision when utilizing your project management team to support Lean improvement projects. Strive for an ongoing improvement process.

Motivating the Team

Design ownership resides with the team and its leadership and not with the project manager, the Lean expert, or the consultant. The team must believe in the project and must feel pride and a sense of accomplishment.

Empower, engage, and be engaged. Improving a process is a lot of work. Utilizing the right methodology and team can make it so much easier. This is why you have a team, with the ability to take on these challenges beyond their routine work. Make it fun and rewarding.

Resolving Issues

The VSM listed all the action items required to implement changes and resolve issues. Some of the actions items have been successfully addressed already. Some others, although very important, encountered major delays and required constant follow-up.

Follow through and commit to resolving issues as promised. Accountability and a high level of credibility are essential. Leadership is required to ensure progress and to prevent a return to old habits.

CONCLUSION

The culture of Lean Thinking is a necessary foundation for any enterprise. This involves more than just the elimination of waste and the creation of value. Lean Thinking offers a method for making things better, all the time and for everybody.

Many organizations are investing time, money, and resources (internal and external) to improve their services and get from point A to B as fast and as efficiently as possible. Although this may be necessary at times, it does not create a Lean culture. In a Lean culture, each team member continuously tries to improve and strives for excellence in all endeavors, ensuring a high level of job satisfaction.

I'm privileged to have had the opportunity to help OML move to a new state-of-the art facility in 2006 and to have overseen the commencement of its Lean journey in 2007. OML has grasped the power and value of Lean, and it understands its contribution to the organization and operation, clients, employees, and bottom line. It made a strategic decision to apply Lean Thinking throughout its enterprise. The start of the OML journey was impressive and many processes have been improved very successfully already. A high level of dedication to this new way of thinking has been noticed and future direction is provided and ensured.

8

Improving Accommodation and Organizational Arrangements at an Outpatient Antenatal Clinic

Brendan Murphy
Mid Western Regional Hospital, Ennis, Ireland

PROJECT BACKGROUND

Following a request from hospital management, we undertook a review using a Lean in Healthcare approach in the outpatient antenatal clinic in the Mid Western Regional Hospital, Ennis, Ireland, in early 2008. The clinic is managed as an outreach clinic by visiting staff from the Mid Western Regional Maternity (MWRM) Hospital, which is located approximately forty kilometers away. Staff had been expressing concern about the perceived inadequacy of clinical rooms in the outpatient area and the poor availability of efficient ultrasound scanning facilities at this clinic, which is held each Wednesday afternoon.

It was agreed with the hospital managers that the priority focus for the review would be the accommodation issue, but comments would be made on equipment and other elements as appropriate. The review was led by the organization development and design unit of the Health Service Executive (HSE), which is located in Limerick, Ireland. The agreed terms of reference were:

> To review and put forward proposals for improvement for the accommodation and organizational arrangements at the outpatient antenatal clinic, paying particular attention to patient safety, confidentiality, and comfort issues.

──────────────

IMPLEMENTING LEAN

We held interviews with hospital management to establish some background information and to understand the issues from their perspective. We also made a preliminary visit to the clinic to meet staff, and to establish information on duties performed, reporting relationships, review layout, and general accommodation. Staff were invited to comment on current working arrangements, existing problems, and potential solutions. We outlined the Lean approach, pointing out the value and indeed necessity for staff and client involvement in the exercise, as well as the benefits of targeting the entire patient journey.

Administration staff were requested to extract a range of clinic statistics so we could explore the throughput and trends over a period of time.

In agreement with clinic staff, we decided to begin a study program to assist a review of general process flows, working arrangements, accommodation, and workloads. This included:

- Designing a staff self-recording form to provide information on patient name, time of arrival, and time of leaving each intervention. This enabled the review team and clinic staff to produce process and current state maps.
- Designing a patient survey questionnaire to provide patients with the opportunity to comment on a range of topics, including journey information, clinic accommodation, waiting times, and the appointment system.
- Undertaking an observation analysis to monitor the general "ebb and flow" of clinic activity and facilitate interaction with clinic staff.

We used a voice of the customer (VOC) approach to gather input from all stakeholders and clearly identify their requirements. The review team and selected staff analyzed the survey results to critically examine accommodation issues, clinic procedures, and documentation.

In conjunction with the clinic staff, we decided to focus on four distinct but interrelated topics:

- Clinic accommodation
- The appointment system

- Chart management
- Clinic procedures

Accommodation Findings

Figure 8.1 shows a plan of the outpatient department (OPD) at the beginning of the exercise, identifying the location of the various rooms. Only four offices and one filing room (shaded) are not occupied by antenatal clinic staff.

FIGURE 8.1
Layout of the outpatient department.

The survey highlighted quality of accommodation as a key issue. A critical examination of the information collected revealed a number of issues.

Clinic Rooms

We noted the following issues with the clinic rooms:

- Room 4 (large room 4.6 × 6.5 m) was congested at times with patients, partners, children, midwives, and nurses. There were often fifteen to seventeen people at any one time.
- Patient interviews, bloods, and urines all took place in the one room. There was no privacy or comfort. Also, this raised some health and safety issues.
- Student midwives occupied whatever room was available to record history.
- The plaster room was not appropriate for patient history recording.
- Other clinic rooms were in good condition and spacious.
- Social workers had no accommodation; interviews were conducted in the hall with no privacy.

Waiting Rooms

We noted the following issues with the waiting rooms:

- The main room was full most of the time; it was very stuffy and had poor ventilation.
- There was a mixture of patients, partners, and children.
- Partners were often sitting, while other patients were standing.
- Seating was basic but satisfactory.
- The six small sub-waiting areas were useful, but they had no signage or reading materials.
- There was a hot beverage dispenser, but no snacks or water nearby. Also, there was little reading material.
- The TV was too small, positioned high up, and on mute.
- Patient survey showed unhappiness with accommodation.

Reception

We noted the following issues with reception:

- There was a lot of crowding at the window, caused by patients arriving and leaving. This led to confusion.
- There was no privacy for patients being asked questions by the receptionist.
- General signage was not good.
- Shelving was not ideally located or labeled.
- Staff frequently entered this small area to collect charts.
- There was a general "cluttered" feel about the office.

Unstructured sessions between the review team and clinic staff generated a lot of open thinking, enabling everyone to build on each other's ideas. We explored logic and viability in depth.

Clinic Rooms

Outpatient procedures should be designed to cause clients the minimum amount of waiting, inconvenience, or embarrassment. A contributing factor in this aspiration is the need for adequate consulting and examination room accommodation and efficient arrangements within the consulting rooms.

The group examined the current state maps in depth, using brainstorming and cause-and-effect analysis techniques to explore possible solutions. When discussing flow, we advised staff that it is important to challenge any division in job roles and responsibilities.

Two alternative scenarios were presented:

- Explore the potential for obtaining additional clinic space within the OPD for the antenatal service.
- Set up a protocol that arranges for new clients to be seen for their first visit in the main maternity hospital.

Regarding the first scenario, we established that there was a short-term and medium-term potential for availing of extra accommodation, which involved freeing up an office when its current occupier retired, relocating two secretaries, and hiring a portacabin in the interim period.

Regarding the second scenario, a number of findings emerged very quickly from the group. There were a number of factors in favor of arranging for new clients to be seen in the main maternity hospital:

- Good consulting facilities
- More comfort for clients and families
- Health and safety enhancements
- Improved privacy
- Excellent standard of equipment
- No repeat scans needed because of poor images
- Scanning would now be carried out by experienced radiographers
- Less waiting time and shorter clinic time
- More doctor and nursing satisfaction
- Improved chart preparation
- Fewer staff traveling from the main hospital
- Freed up accommodation for return clients
- Improved flow of work
- Less pressure on scanning equipment
- Precedent set by other clinics in the region and working well
- 87 percent of clinic clients have access to a car (as per patient survey)

However, there were a number of factors in favor of having new clients continue to attend the current antenatal clinic:

- Many clients would have to travel farther for the first visit.
- The capacity in the main maternity hospital would need to be reviewed.
- Clinic frequency in the main hospital would need to be reviewed.
- The availability and capacity of the radiographers in the hospital would have to be assessed.

Setting the main arguments of quality scanning, privacy, health and safety, accommodation enhancements, and the existing precedent against the arguments for not changing the protocol, we realized that this recommendation required serious consideration.

Discussions have taken place and it is anticipated that this proposal will gain new momentum in the foreseeable future.

In the interim, the office has been freed and a portacabin has been installed, resulting in a significant reduction in congestion, in additional privacy, and in comfort and the elimination of an inappropriate history-taking room.

Waiting Accommodation

General amenities in the main waiting area could be improved by:

- Provision of a larger, more appropriately placed television with a degree of sound or a channel with a scrolling news facility
- Introduction of some light reading material, which also caters for children
- Improving ventilation
- Erecting notices advising visitors to give up their seats to clients of the clinic and to facilitate families to stay together

The implementation of improved waiting room amenities has made a noticeable difference to patient and visitor comfort, achieving a much improved waiting experience for them.

Reception

We recommended that the office layout be examined to improve ergonomic elements. Confidentiality at queuing could also be enhanced by the provision of a simple "Do not cross" line for clients (positioned appropriately on the entrance floor) and the erection of two small panels on either side of the window. An office spring cleaning and the erection of advisory notices have immediately contributed to a more efficient service.

Staffing in Reception

The basic role of a receptionist is to sort out the client charts as necessary and greet each client on arrival. The receptionist then explains the procedure to the client and shows her where to wait. An experienced receptionist was needed. One was obtained and the impact has been immediate in terms of enhancing the patient experience while attracting positive comments from medical and nursing staff.

Figure 8.2 shows the potential changes to room occupancy.

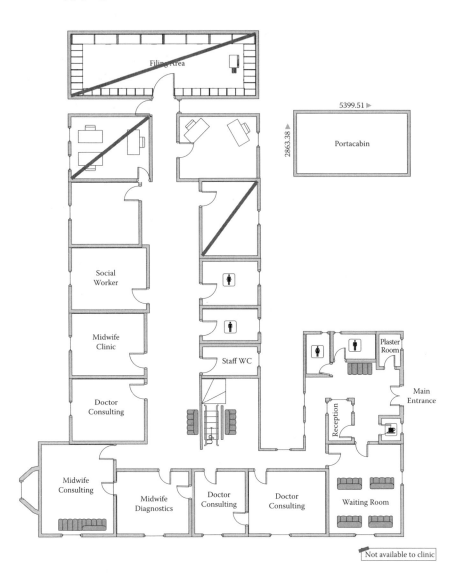

FIGURE 8.2
Proposed layout of the outpatient department.

The Appointment System

Patients for an antenatal clinic can be issued with an appointment following:

- A previous outpatient visit
- A letter sent by the general practitioner (GP)

TABLE 8.1

Appointment Times for New Patients

	New Patients	
Time	9/01/08	16/01/08
1345	3	3
1410	3	3
1435	2	2
1500	2	2
1525	2	2
Total called to clinic	12	12
Did not attend (DNA)	1	0

The clinic caters to both new and review patients. Appointment times for each were issued during the survey dates (Table 8.1 and Table 8.2).

After analyzing all the information collected, we summarized the findings as follows:

- Appointments were issued between 1345 and 1525 for new patients and between 1400 and 1605 for review patients. During the study period an average of twelve new patients and fifty-three review patients were called each week to the clinic.
- The bulk of patients were called to early slots, which can lead to congestion in reception and waiting areas (87.5 percent in first hour and a quarter and 12.5 percent in last forty-five minutes).
- Some patients came early in the hope of getting away early, while a number of patients were not seen in appointment order.
- Clinic preparation time was very tight because of the early appointment times and staff arrival time.
- The first patient was seldom seen before 1410, although she may have arrived some forty minutes earlier.
- Appointment times were not given to the clients leaving the clinic after 1705 if the receptionist had gone home.
- Appointment information was often insufficient because of the quality of GP referrals.
- A number of new clients request the main maternity hospital for the first visit.

The group agreed that the main aim of any clinic should be to create a steady flow of patients through the system at a steady rate. It was vital

TABLE 8.2

Appointment Times for Review Patients

	Review Patients	
Time	9/01/08	16/01/08
1400	4	4
1405	4	4
1410	4	4
1415	2	2
1420	3	1
1430	—	4
1435	4	2
1440	1	1
1445	4	2
1450	4	4
1455	—	4
1500	4	4
1505	—	5
1510	4	4
1515	4	5
1520	1	4
1525	1	1
1530	1	1
1540	1	1
1550	—	1
1600	—	—
1605	2	—
Total called to clinic	48	58
Did not attend (DNA)	6	2

that clinic start and finish times, appointment times, and staff start and finish times should be coordinated to ensure the smooth running of the clinic. Queues form when demand exceeds capacity. All the evidence in this survey and in others showed that clients had to wait in OPD much too long. Much of this waiting was unnecessary. Following a concerted brainstorming session, it became clear that a new appointments scheme was needed as a priority.

TABLE 8.3

How to Diagnose What's Wrong with Your Appointment System

Client's Waiting Time	Doctor's Waiting Time	What's Going Wrong?
Low	Occurs through clinic, especially at start	Doctor arriving before first clients or consultation time has become shorter
High throughout clinic	Nil	Doctor arriving after first clients or too many clients at start
Increases throughout clinic	Less and less likely throughout clinic	Appointment rate too fast
Decreases throughout clinic	More and more likely throughout clinic	Appointment rate too slow
Average constant throughout clinic but some may wait very long times	Some occasional waits	Miscellaneous operational problems with, for example, ambulance clients, preclinical procedures, variable consulting times, etc.
Low throughout clinic	Occurs occasionally	Nothing—you've got it about right!

We had to consider three main points when designing the scheme:

- The time of the first appointment
- The number of appointments given in the clinic
- How appointments are distributed throughout the clinic

A total review of the clinic profile and scheduling has now taken place and proposals have been adopted. There is a noticeable reduction in congestion and a significant improvement in client flow through the clinic. Waiting times have been reduced and appointments are given on departure, adding to a better experience for the patient while reducing administrative elements for clinic staff.

A literature review revealed a template for advice on "How to diagnose what is wrong with your appointment scheme,"[*] and this was used as a basis for developing a new scheme. A copy of the template is included in Table 8.3 and will be used by staff in the future to monitor the relationship among the appointment system, client's waiting time, and doctor's waiting time.

---

[*] Department of Health and Social Security: Operational Research Service. Clearing your clinic—A new approach to cutting outpatient waiting times.

Healthcare Record Management

The group and other staff discussed chart management issues at length, concentrating on the experiences of clients holding their own charts, lost charts, lost information, completing demographic information in the waiting room, chasing information, file sorting procedures, and so on.

The dual chart system raised a number of concerns, especially with regard to information security if a chart is lost or damaged and the noted absence of electronic backup. As a result, we recommended that we should reassess the value of having clients hold their own chart and that we adopt a consistent approach for all clients in the hospital network. A focused survey is examining this issue in full.

We also recommended that pigeonholes should be labeled as appropriate to clearly highlight their contents. Additionally, we deemed it useful to explore the potential of inserting fixed dividers to help staff to select the right chart as per appointment time and return it to the appropriate place. These recommendations are now bearing fruit and dramatically minimizing errors and ensuring fair play. It was noted that all the users of the patient administration system (PAS) for this clinic were accessing the system using the same username and password. Individual usernames and passwords are now in use and security has been improved.

Clinic Procedures

A staff self-recording exercise enabled us to produce a map following the patient to identify value and non-value activities within the clinic. It was important to establish start and finish points in advance, and the group selected patient arrival at the clinic and patient check out, respectively.

The amount of waiting time for each intervention could now be quantified for each category of staff. Cycle times could also be calculated for each treatment or consultation type. Analysis of waiting times revealed that new patients were waiting a total of seventy minutes for attention during the clinic, while review patients could expect to wait an average of sixty minutes for attention.

For illustration purposes, the current and future process maps are shown in Figure 8.3 and Figure 8.4.

To achieve a good understanding of the patient flow in the clinic, we also created a current state map. This enabled us to analyze the process

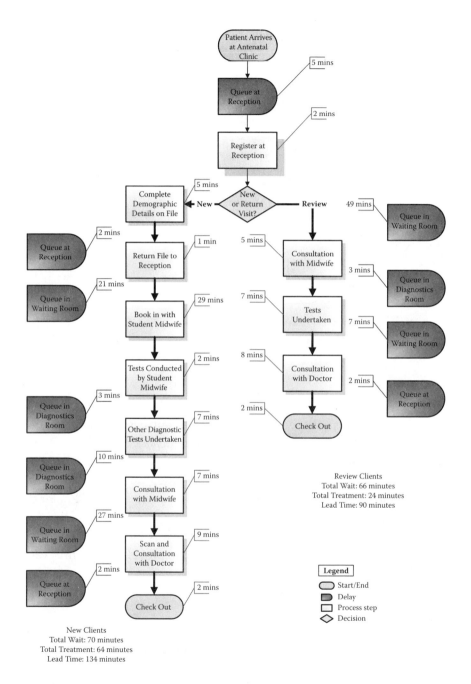

FIGURE 8.3
Current process map.

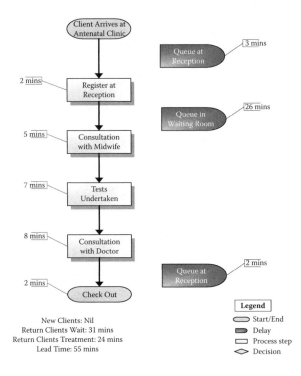

FIGURE 8.4

Future process map.

and identify the steps that do not add value. The current state map for new patients is shown in Figure 8.5 for illustration purposes.

The preliminary visit enabled the group to ascertain the main steps in the process, which followed the three streams depending on the nature of the clinic visit: as a new patient, as a review patient, or as a "low risk" patient for a midwife-only clinic.

We also had to calculate the Takt time, which is essentially the client demand rate. In this instance, the group focused on each of the three categories of client above.

Takt time was calculated as follows:

$$\frac{\text{Actual operating time for the clinic}}{\text{Customer requirement for the clinic}}$$

$$\text{New} = \frac{210 \text{ (no breaks)}}{12} = 17.5 \text{ min}$$

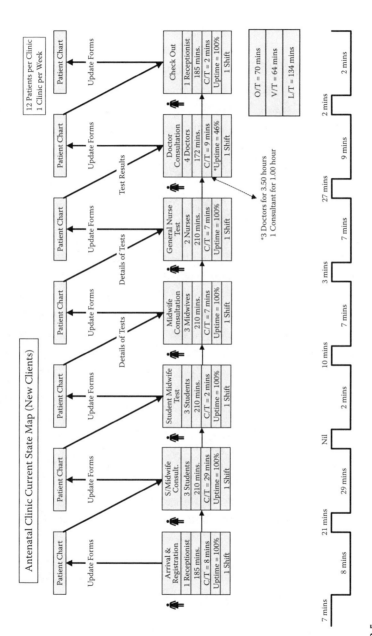

FIGURE 8.5
Current state map.

$$\text{Review} = \frac{210 \text{ (no breaks)}}{53} = 4 \text{ min}$$

$$\text{Midwives' clinic} = \frac{180 \text{ (no breaks)}}{10} = 18 \text{ min}$$

To meet customer demand, new patients need to be treated every seventeen and a half minutes, review patients every four minutes, and patients for the midwife clinic every eighteen minutes.

At the group meetings, the doctors in particular expressed their surprise at the extent of the waiting times, admitting that they had not realized how long and often clients had to wait! Expressions such as "Who have we really devised the system for?" emerged.

As advised earlier, the group identified the second scenario (i.e., using the main maternity hospital) as having the most potential, and the target was to analyze the steps and determine which ones added value and which ones did not.

From the outset, the one major difference would be the elimination in its entirety of the current state map for new patients in Ennis if they are all redirected to the main maternity hospital. This would bring the following benefits:

- Opportunity time (non-value) of seventy minutes is gone.
- Value-added time of sixty-four minutes is gone.
- Ten fewer patients would be presenting at the clinic.
- Student midwives, midwives, and doctors could potentially be redeployed.
- Less demand would be made on the receptionist.
- Less demand would be made on the waiting and clinic accommodation.

Regarding the current state map for return clients, the group examined the value-added and non-value-added elements and also produced a future state map. Opportunity time and value-added time were directly and indirectly affected by a number of elements:

- Removal of new clients from the clinic
- Potential to start the clinic at an appropriate time
- Redesign of the appointment system
- A focus on encouraging clients to come on time
- Separation of treatment and consultation tasks in room 4 by using room 3 for diagnostics
- A more efficient reception service
- Better chart management
- Enhanced availability of doctor and nursing staff

The impact of the above on opportunity time would be a reduction from sixty-six to thirty-one minutes initially, with scope for further improvements through client education.

With regard to value-added time, it was estimated that this would remain the same at twenty-four minutes, giving therefore an overall lead-time of fifty-five minutes (a reduction of 39 percent).

The group then turned its attention to reviewing the current state map for the midwives' clinic and developed a future state map, focusing on the following considerations:

- Introduce a new appointments system
- Start the clinic on time
- Use an education process to get clients to come on time
- Take two more patients onto the service

The impact of the above would reduce opportunity time from thirty-four to ten minutes, while value-added time would stay the same. Total lead time would now be thirty minutes.

At this point, the group reviewed the Takt time for each client type and set it against the cycle times. It was noted that Takt time would be eliminated for the new client category, would remain at four minutes for review clients, and would reduce to fifteen minutes for midwife-only clients (recalculated at 180/12). This represents an increase in client throughput for the same attendance time.

RESULTS AND LESSONS LEARNED

The Way Forward

The exercise has identified a number of recommendations for improving the service. To maximize gain from the review, we proposed the following implementation plan:

1. The report will be issued and a meeting will be organized.
2. Recommendations will be separated into easily achievable wins and longer targets.
3. Longer implementation targets should be prioritized according to business objectives and agreement reached on resourcing issues.
4. We proposed that the review group and survey staff be invited to review progress within six months, via discussions, interviews, and walkthroughs.

Overall Conclusions

Improvements can be made to any service area by an approach that steps back and records the current state, critically analyzes this, and then develops a future state for the benefit of clients and staff. Known as the employment of a Lean philosophy, this approach can encourage all staff to look at how clients and materials flow through a system to unlock bottlenecks and inefficiencies. It was important to focus on a bottom line, which was to streamline the clients' journey through the clinic while attempting to improve safety, confidentiality, and comfort issues. Staff are best placed to know what adds value to their daily working lives and by challenging potential inefficiencies in conjunction with the other main players (i.e., our clients), it is possible to make a significant difference.

9

Improving Wait Times at a Medical Oncology Unit

Carlos F. Pinto
HRVP Medical Oncology Unit, Taubate, Brazil

PROJECT BACKGROUND

HRVP and Medical Oncology Unit Background

The Regional Hospital from Vale do Paraiba (HRVP), located in Taubate, seventy-five miles from São Paulo, is a public hospital with 300 beds. It provides specialized treatment: cancer (surgery, chemotherapy, and radiation therapy), cardiac and vascular surgery, neurosurgery, renal substitutive therapy, and transplants. It is also a teaching unit for medical students and interns. In 2007, HRVP was nominated Public Hospital of the Year.

In 2000, our group started a partnership with HRVP and we assumed the activities of the cancer unit there. The medical oncology unit at HRVP (HRVP-MOU) is a multiprofessional center with 120 to 150 appointments daily. More than fifty patients receive chemo or hormonal treatment for cancer, as inpatients or outpatients each day.

The physical area comprises the following:

- Eight exam rooms
- A group and family room
- Social worker and nurse facilities
- Ambulatory chemotherapy facilities for twenty-one patients
- Offices
- Waiting rooms
- Support areas (cleaning, archives, etc.)

More than forty collaborators work with us: physicians, psychologists, social workers, pharmacists, nurses, and office and support staff.

IMPLEMENTING LEAN

HRVP-MOU Front Desk

I decided to start the Lean project at our most challenging area: the front desk at HRVP-MOU. Patients come from surrounding cities to the hospital. They sometimes travel two or more hours and may arrive much earlier than the appointed time. It is difficult not to attend to someone who arrives early.

The front desk, called the arrival and registration (A&R) area, is a workstation area with three attendants. They coordinate:

- All patients' arrivals
- Medical, nurse, pharmacist, and psychology appointments
- Group activities
- Chemotherapy treatment schedules and insurance coverage (public or private)
- Treatment approvals
- Pain resources
- Social and legal support
- Information
- Prescription refills, and so forth

Patients and professionals have noted the following problems with the A&R area:

- Significant waiting times
- Exam result delays
- Incomplete data sheets
- Unbalanced workload
- Uncoordinated access to treatment or appointments
- Time wasted searching for information that should be readily available

TABLE 9.1

The Relevance of the A&R to All MOU Processes

	A&R	Assessment	Exam Rooms	Chemo	Pharmacy	Back Office
Medical appointment	X	X	X	X		X
Psychology appointment	X	X	X			
Blood test results	X	X				X
X-ray, CT, US approval/ appointment	X					X
X-ray results	X					X
Treatment approval/ appointment	X			X		X
Social work	X		X			
Pharmacist appointment	X				X	
Nurse appointment	X	X		X		
Information	X					X
Pain and palliative care	X	X	X		X	
Legal support, reports, etc.	X					X

Morale is low, and workers are usually tired and unsatisfied with their results. Small gains in this area would result in significant process improvement.

Table 9.1 shows how the A&R area relates to our other activities. Managing medical appointments takes up more than 70 percent of the A&R time.

Getting Started

The Lean team came from the quality office, with additional team members from A&R. The final team was very large, but we'd decided to allow everyone interested in Lean to participate.

The initial Lean training was based on the Green Belt student material and material from the Lean Institute, Brazil. I gave two Lean presentations and also conducted a workshop on Lean. The team received some 5S training and the weekly quality meeting was used to organize and set up the value stream map.

Figure 9.1 shows the MOU patient journey. The journey involved several steps, including the following:

- Patient arrival
- Setting up or retrieving charts
- Searching for blood and x-ray results
- Assessing the patient for blood pressure, drugs in use, recent side effects, or other relevant information
- Organizing treatment
- Discharging the patient

We did not evaluate the medical consultation process; we just calculated its Takt time. We also did not evaluate the chemotherapy times—they varied too much to be of use to this project. (We decided to use the chemotherapy area for another VSM in the future.)

Current State Map

We first had to identify any opportunities for improvement. To do this, we calculated the shift times and personnel available. This enabled us to map the current state.

I decided not to allow people to modify the process immediately. They were given the time to reflect on the current state before changing it. After we mapped the current state, some solutions were obvious and easy to implement.

For example, it was obvious that the A&R personnel had an excessive workload. The spaghetti diagrams (Figure 9.2) revealed how difficult the A&R daily activity was, and how confused the patient flow was. We later discovered that some other workers had free time to share with the A&R attendants.

Table 9.2 shows the workload data at A&R. It shows that 248 duties were assigned to the A&R area on the first shift; this is a clear overload, with a significant impact on the Takt time. Table 9.3 shows the calculations.

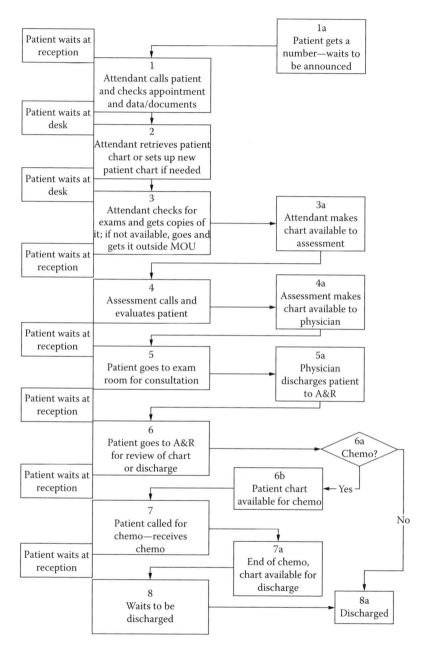

FIGURE 9.1
The patient journey.

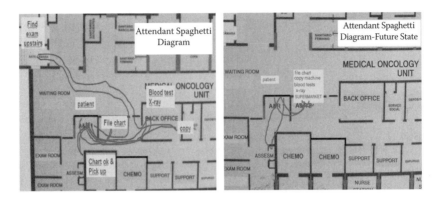

FIGURE 9.2
Spaghetti diagrams showing the current and future states.

The completed current state map (Figure 9.3) revealed a lead time of 112 minutes for any patient arriving for an appointment. There was made up of 37 minutes of value-added time and 75 minutes of non-value-added time. To improve the process, we identified at least four possible rapid improvement Kaizen events and developed a 5S activity.

Improvement Expectations

Quantitative

We could reduce lead time and improve patient satisfaction and flow by:

- Improving workload balance at the area
- Implementing SMED for changeover time
- Removing unnecessary steps and waste (by reducing chart and exam searches, transportation or movement, and repetitive work)

Expected results:

- Optimize V/T by 30 percent or 11 minutes
- Reduce O/T by 25 percent or 18 minutes
- Reduce the 583 minutes (nine hours) daily wasted

TABLE 9.2

Current Workload at A&R

	Source of Data	1st Shift Demand
Medical appointments		
New	60 new patients/month (a)	3
Return	1,550 appoint/month (2/3 at this shift) (b)	50
Other appointments	500 appoint/month (c)	15
Support activities: information for visitors, relatives, etc.	Data collected for assignment	25
Phone calls (internal + external)	2,500 calls/month	60
Treatment approval/exam appointment	Chemo per day	27
Patient discharge	All appointments (a + b + c)	68
Total A&R patients duties 1st shift		248

TABLE 9.3

Takt Time Calculations

TAKT time calculations for medical appointment based on 1st shift demand:

3 physicians work ($\times$) 4 hours shift (–) 30 minutes break: $3 \times (4 \times 60) - (3 \times 30) = 630$ min
TAKT appointment = 630 min/53 appointments = 12 min per patient

TAKT time calculations for A&R area based on 1st shift demand:

3 attendants work ($\times$) 4 hours shift (–) 30 minutes break: $3 \times (4 \times 60) - (3 \times 30) = 630$ min
TAKT A&R = 630 min/248 patients duties = 3 min per patient

Qualitative

We could bring about the following qualitative improvements:

- Waste elimination, by better utilizing resources and removing unnecessary steps
- Improved safety and productivity, using 5S
- Improved flow, streamlining all steps from push to pull systems
- Continuous improvement, using the nine freed hours for value-added activities, such as patient education, medical and nurse care, and Lean Thinking

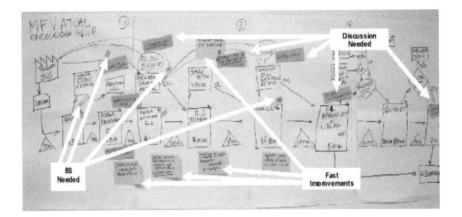

FIGURE 9.3
Current state map (photo).

Problem Analysis

After completing the current state map, we were able to easily spot the problems and identify some solutions. Table 9.4 lists the problems, the tools to be used, the solutions, and the numbered Kaizen events related to them.

The future state suggested that we use a supermarket for blood tests, x-rays, and charts. We could also level the workload and pull activities between A&R and assessment.

We created a Kanban system to pull patients to chemotherapy; patients who had a previous appointment could skip a step. This reduced workload at A&R and simplified the process for some patients. Figure 9.4 shows the future state diagram.

New Data from the Future State Map

After completing the future state map, new measurements were available where we could expect significant improvements. One of the most important conclusions was that these improvements would come without any cost or investment.

Table 9.5 shows the current and future workload at A&R after the Kaizen events. This new workload also improved the Takt times for the A&R area and medical appointments, as seen in Table 9.5, Table 9.6, and Figure 9.5.

TABLE 9.4

Problem Analysis and Solutions

Step	Problem	Opportunity to	Solution	Kaizen No.
1	Patient registering	Reduce	Redesign area: move	1
2	process has	movement	equipment and	1
	excessive	Elimination/	furniture	
	movement and	combination	SMED + Supermarket:	
	steps: chart and	of steps	the day before the	
	copies in another	Standard Work	appointment, set up	
	room; x-rays in	SMED	charts (copies, blood	
	another unit—	Leveling	tests, x-rays), do one	
	patient waits at		full roundtrip daily,	
	desk		not 15 or 25 daily	
3	Attendants have too		Rearrange duties to	1 and 2
	many duties		other personnel at 1st	
			shift: some personnel	
			have free time late	
			afternoon; we just	
			move duties to	
			afternoon to create	
			more time in the	
			morning for leveling	
			activities	
4	This activity breaks	Leveling	Distribute some	2
	the flow twice, it	Pulling	activity from front	
	can be partially		desk to assessment	
	pulled		Pull patients from	
			admittance to	
			assessment	
			immediately	
5	New patients wait	Leveling	Appointment for new	4
	up to hours for the		patients only at end of	
	appointment		the morning or early	
			afternoon	
5	Delays due to exams	Flow	Signaling (kanban) to	1 and 3
	not available or	improvement	assessment who is	
	patients not ready	Pull and	attending and	
	for consultation	signaling	establishing continu-	
		Elimination/	ous flow for these	
		combination	patients (some patients	
		of steps	with available	
			physicians wait for	
			assessment evaluation)	

(continued on next page)

TABLE 9.4 (continued)

Problem Analysis and Solutions

Step	Problem	Opportunity to	Solution	Kaizen No.
6	Patients wait for an approved procedure or discharge	Kanban and elimination/ combination of steps	Kanban for patients with approved procedures to move straight to the chemo area, leaving this step to patients with pending approvals	1 and 3
7	Patient time inside chemo area can be combined to discharge	Elimination/ combination of steps	Discharge patient inside chemo, while finishing its infusions	5
8	Many patients have to wait to be discharged			5

RESULTS AND LESSONS LEARNED

The Takt time comparisons clearly show the benefits for the A&R area; the Takt time was reduced from fourteen to five minutes. Almost 90 percent of what we proposed was achieved.

The patient journey was also improved, with fewer queues and steps. Table 9.7 compares the initial proposals and final achievements, whereas Figure 9.6 shows the future state patient journey. Each planned Kaizen event became an action plan, and they were integrated into our audit process.

Action Plan

We developed five major actions (5S + Kaizen events), using a mixture of our previous PDCA model and the new experimental A3 model (Figure 9.7, Table 9.8, Table 9.9, and Table 9.10). These plans became our value stream map. The final phase of this value stream map is to standardize the work based on this new design. We expect to fully incorporate Lean Thinking into our quality processes.

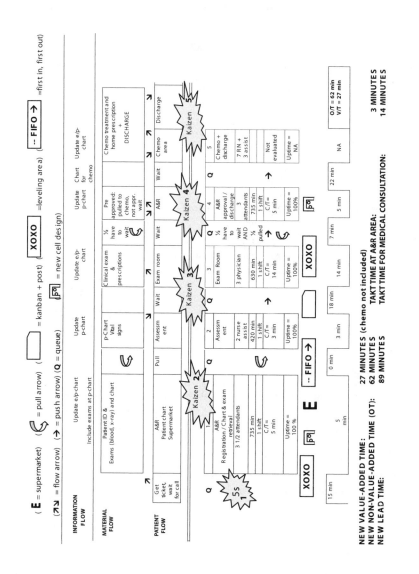

FIGURE 9.4
Future state map implementation.

TABLE 9.5

Workload Comparisons between Current and Future States

		Current State	Future State
	Source of Data	1st Shift	1st Shift
Medical appointments:			
New *(moved to afternoon)*	60 new patients/month	3	0
Return	1,550 appointments/ month (2/3 at this shift)	50	50
Other appointments	500 appointments/ month	15	15
Support activities: information for visitors, relatives, etc.	Data collected for assignment	25	25
Phone calls (internal + external)	2,500 calls/month	60	60
Treatment approval/exam appointment	Chemo per day *(reduced ½, preapproved)*	27	15
Patient discharge	All appointments *(minus chemo patient discharged inside chemo = 27)*	68	41
Total A&R patients duties 1st shift		248	206

TABLE 9.6

New Takt Time Calculations

Included one new attendant with ½ shift available time

3½ attendants ($\times$) 4 hours shift (–) 30 min break: $3\frac{1}{2} \times (4 \times 60) - (3\frac{1}{2} \times 30) = 735$ min

Takt = 735 min/206 patients duties = 4 minutes per patient

New TAKT for medical appointments

3 physicians ($\times$) 4 hours shift (–) 30 minutes break: $3 \times (4 \times 60) - (3 \times 30) = 630$ min

Takt = 630 min/50 appointments = 13 minutes per patient

CONCLUDING REMARKS

The initial experience with Lean Thinking at HRVP-MOU was very encouraging. We were particularly impressed by how simple the most

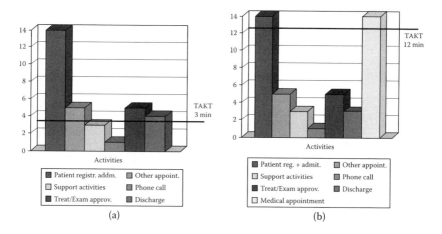

FIGURE 9.5

Current state Takt times for (a) all activities and (b) medical appointments.

TABLE 9.7

VSM Results

	VSM		Improvement			
			Minute		(%)	
	Current	Future	Proposed	Future	Proposed	Future
Value-added time	37	27	−11	−10	30	28
Non-value-added time	75	62	−18	−13	25	18
Lead time	112	87	−29	−23	25	23
Takt A&R area	3	4	—	+1	—	25
Takt medical appointment	12	13	—	+1	—	8

beneficial solution (the supermarket) was. Not only was it simple, it added no cost (except the time spent thinking and moving the furniture and equipment). Attendants are proud of the improvements they were able to create, and obviously they are happy with the lighter workload. Earlier complaints about excessive jobs and the need for more collaborators are completely gone. People are now asking about flow improvement, not resource improvement. The area selected was the right one: it had a lot of waste, a lot of people, a lot of work, and a lot of flow. We are genuinely excited with the results.

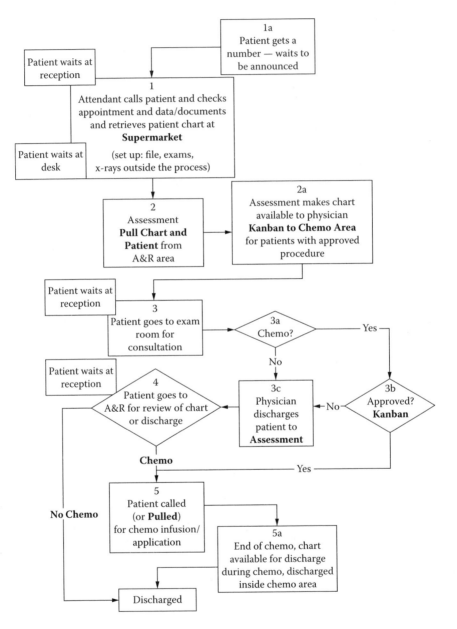

FIGURE 9.6
The future state patient journey.

Issue: **VALUE STREAM PLAN**

Background:

Target condition:

Current condition:

Problem analysis:

ACTION PLAN:

#	What	Who	Why	How	Outcome	D	J	F	M	A	M	J	J	A	S	O

Check:

Follow-up:

Signatures: _____   Authors: _____   Version and date: _____

FIGURE 9.7
A3 for VSM and A&R.

TABLE 9.8

Action Plan 1

#	What	Who	Why	How	Outcome	December 1	2	3	4	January 1	2	3	4	February 1	2	3	4
1	Team setup for 5S	Carlos	Experience in 5S training	Meetings at unit training PowerPoint, discussions	Compromised and competent team	P											
1	Familiarization with 5S		Be familiar			P											
1	Managers training					P											
1	Define target area	5s Team	Locate where it has more impact	Meeting for area allocation	Area to work: A&R + back office + assessment and exam room	P											
1	Photograph area		Identify benefits visually in the future	Take pictures before and after the 5S	Identify benefits visually in the future	P											

	Task	Owner	Action	Detail	5S											
1	Sort and set in order		Identify unnecessary equipment, activity, etc.	One shift for the activity	2S	D										C
	Define staging area		Store material not clearly unnecessary	Define area		D										
1	Shine		Clean area	One shift for the activity	3S	D										
1	Standardize		Standardize 5S and sustain it	Standardized work	4S	D D						C		C		
1	Sustain			Standardized work	5S	D			C		C	C				
1	Cleaning plan for sustaining			New photo session			P									
				Clean and ordered workplace												
1	Meeting with audit team for internal audit	Team + audit team		Planning and including it in our routine (internal audit planning)					P	P CA						A

TABLE 9.9

Action Plans 2 and 3

#	What	Who	Why	How	Outcome	January 1	January 2	January 3	January 4	February 1	February 2	February 3	February 4	March 1	March 2	March 3	March 4
2	Combine steps 1, 2, and 3 of the current state map	Team + personnel	The activity with the worst performance to Takt	Meeting at area for design	Eliminate steps 2 and 3 combining to 1	P	D										
2	Create a supermarket for chart and exams	Personnel	Reduce movement to seek for blood tests, x-rays, copies	SMED: get scheduled patients and 1 day before seek for exams in the afternoon, make copies, where time is available	Reduce time from 14 to 5 minutes	D	D										
2	Reallocate copy machine and charts	Personnel	Reduce unnecessary movement	Moving furniture		D											
2	Evaluate improvement	Personnel + team	Check improvement	New measurements			CA										

2	Divide activity in two	Personnel	Many activities are not related to appointments	Using area available to create to work cells	Improve Takt time for A&R	P			
2	Activity 1 (act 1) definition and mapping	Personnel	Define what duties attendants will do	Analyzing activity, queries, phone calls, etc.	Standardized work	P			
2	Allocate personnel to activity 2 (act 2) at A&R (½ shift)	Personnel manager	Define what information and approval attendants will do	Analyzing activity, queries, phone calls, etc.	Standardized work	P			
2	Create continuous flow to assessment area	Personnel at A&R and assessment	Eliminate patient queue and circulation using (– FIFO →)	Nurse assistant will contact patient at front desk for assessment (pull and – FIFO →)	Eliminate 1 step and queue	D	D	DCA	

(continued on next page)

TABLE 9.9 (continued)

Action Plans 2 and 3

#	What	Who	Why	How	Outcome	January 1	2	3	4	February 1	2	3	4	March 1	2	3	4
3	Identify patient with pre-approved procedure	Nurse assistant + attendant at act 2	Signalize to chemo and approval/ discharge area (colored area) patient pre-approved	Evaluating chart/ prescription and signaling it with colored tag/area (kanban); define colored areas							PD						
3	Kanban to move patient out of exam room to chemo	Nurse assistant	Eliminate queue and step	Using kanban previously assigned to chart							DCA						
2+3	Evaluate and audit	Team + audit team	Standardize work and evaluate result	Internal audit	For plan 2 and 3: Eliminate 3 steps and 2 queues, improve Takt												

TABLE 9.10

Action Plans 4 and 5

#	What	Who	Why	How	Outcome	January 1	January 2	January 3	January 4	February 1	February 2	February 3	February 4	March 1	March 2	March 3	March 4
4	Reorganize schedule to move new patients to afternoon	Team + A&R personnel	Improve Takt time for consultation, moving patients not in chemo to later in the morning or at afternoon agenda	Reviewing agenda and leveling activity	Improve Takt and reduce long consultations early in the morning	PD	C A										
5	Simplify discharge process from chemo																
5	RN at chemo + attendant at act 2	Eliminate 1 step at end of process	Discharging patient during chemo, at final washout, usually late in the morning or at the afternoon, when attendants have available time	Eliminate 1 step and 1 queue						P D C A							
5	Standardize work		Sustain	Standard operational procedure							C	D	C				
5	Audit	Audit team	Standardize work and evaluate result	Internal audit									C	C	A		
5	Evaluate	All	Check efficiency	New VSM	New Kaizen cycle									C	A		

10

Minimizing the Time from "Cooking Pot to Patient"

Judy-Ann Wybenga
Red Deer Regional Hospital Center, Alberta, Canada

PROJECT BACKGROUND

Organizational Profile

Nutrition and Food Services (NFS) has been a regional department since 1995 and currently provides a full spectrum of clinical nutrition and food services in twenty-one hospitals and care centers across the David Thompson Health Region (DTHR).

The department administrative structure provides regional resources for site operations. It integrates nutrition and food services, site program needs, and planning and administration needs. The NFS administration team is made up of dieticians specializing in healthcare food service administration and clinical nutrition. The responsibility for day-to-day meal service delivery is decentralized to the site level.

The Red Deer Regional Hospital Center (RDRHC) has a centralized, cook–freeze production center. The existing meal delivery system at RDRHC is twenty-seven years old. Both the rethermalization (reheating) and meal delivery equipment need constant maintenance and are showing extreme signs of wear, because of the years of constant use. This system relies on holding rethermalized cooked foods in obsolete hot-holding steam tables. This hot-holding equipment is difficult to manage effectively and does not provide consistently hot meals to the tray line. Portioned meals are placed onto individual trays. These are then transported to nursing units in unheated, poorly protected service carts. Food temperature is retained by using insulated plate bases and domes. Food quality is compromised during the tray assembly process. Also, there are lengthy transfers between each step in the process, and food often waits at the nursing unit before being served to patients.

The goals of this case study were as follows:

- Value stream mapping (VSM) of the current meal delivery system
- Brainstorming on how to minimize the time from "cooking pot to patient"

IMPLEMENTING LEAN

Current VSM for Meal Tray Delivery

RDRHC is a 365-bed acute care hospital built in 1980. NFS delivers meal tray carts to sixteen patient care areas. Meal trays are then delivered by nursing staff to the patient bedside.

Delays between cart arrival and delivery of trays to the bedside have a negative impact on food quality, especially the temperature of the food. Patient satisfaction scores are persistently low regarding food temperatures. Also, food safety concerns arise when hot food is served after a cumulative delay.

The response by nursing to NFS taking over bed-to-bed tray delivery has been positive. NFS can plan the workload to minimize transport time between the kitchen and the bedside. A pilot project could be planned for unit 22, a thirty-six-bed unit.

After meal service, opportunities exist to better manage the workload and flow of carts back to warewashing. For example, one problem is that the turnaround time for meal cleanup can be delayed if nurses do not return the trays to the carts for pick up by NFS.

Improvement Expectations

We could address these problems by:

- Improving the meals by serving them at the most palatable temperature.
- Improving patient satisfaction scores related to appropriateness of food temperatures.
- Validating time and cost of bed-to-bed delivery to achieve correct pay classification of staff. Wages for NFS are $15.42 per hour. Nursing wages range from $16.40 for an attendant to $20.19 per hour for a licensed practical nurse to $35.55 per hour for a registered nurse.
- Decreasing the turnaround time for full meal trays leaving the kitchen and for empty trays returning to warewashing.
- Enabling nurses to focus on meal setup and consumption activities that add value to patients once NFS has delivered the trays.
- Increasing staff empowerment and morale by teaching them how to solve daily problems using Lean methods.
- Enabling staff to utilize their skills and time more efficiently.
- Improving relations with Nursing.

Current Situation

We created process observation forms to gather data on weekday and weekend cart runs. The traffic volume and business in the hospital are markedly different on weekdays compared to the weekend. Collecting data for both permutations of cart delivery helped capture some useful quantitative and qualitative data. We gathered secondary data from direct observation and informal interviews.

The current state map (Figure 10.1) includes all elements of waste identified in each process step. The map outlines the total lead time, opportunity lead time, and Takt time for cart delivery.

Spaghetti diagrams give an indication of travel paths. Photos (Figure 10.2, Figure 10.3, Figure 10.4, and Figure 10.5) reflect the time lost during various stages of the process: waiting for food items, waiting for the elevator, and waiting for nursing staff to deliver meal trays.

The VSM of the process gave us a visual platform from which to plan improvements. The service rate appears to align with customer demand reasonably well, although trays are pushed through the process. The information gained from this preliminary value identification will be

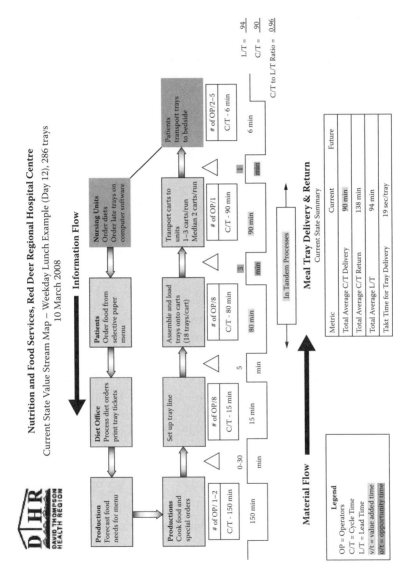

FIGURE 10.1
Current state map.

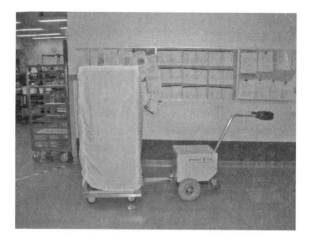

FIGURE 10.2
One cart waiting for its companion before leaving the kitchen.

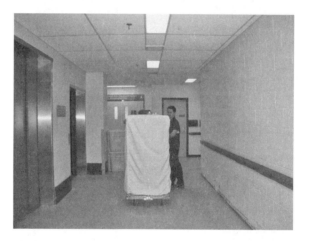

FIGURE 10.3
Cart waiting for the elevator.

used to create a future state map and value stream plan in stage 2 of this assignment.

Future State VSM for Meal Tray Delivery

The initial goal of doing a VSM for the meal tray delivery process was based on the hypothesis that there was an unnecessary waiting time between

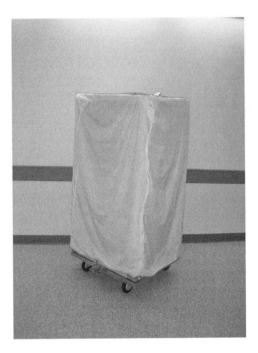

FIGURE 10.4
Cart waiting for delivery to the patient's bedside.

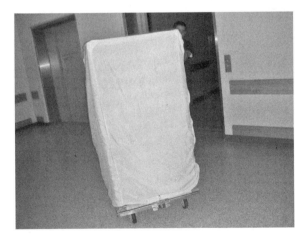

FIGURE 10.5
Post-meal service—cart waiting to return to the dish room via elevator.

tray line meal assembly, cart arrival, and tray delivery to the patient bed-side. However, there were differences between how we thought the process worked, how it should work, and how it actually worked. For example, direct observation of six different meal periods did not show trays sitting idle once they left the kitchen. Moreover, there was limited variance in the time taken by five different employees in completing cart portering tasks.

Delays caused by delivery design limitations (such as transporting food in carts via elevators) were minimal. Nevertheless, the patient satisfaction surveys confirmed that improvement opportunities abounded. It was stressed to the Lean team that what the patients were looking for was safe, hot, nutritious food delivered on time.

Stage 1 results shed light on how to maintain and promote food and temperature quality *before* carts leave the kitchen. Thus, stage 2 focused on maximizing temperature retention and patient satisfaction. This approach is in keeping with the cause-and-effect problem analysis (Figure 10.6).

The project goals were as follows:

- Improving consumption of meals, with foods served at the most palatable temperature, rather than lukewarm
- Improving patient satisfaction scores related to appropriateness of food temperatures
- Decreasing turnaround time for full meal trays
- Validating time and cost of bed-to-bed delivery

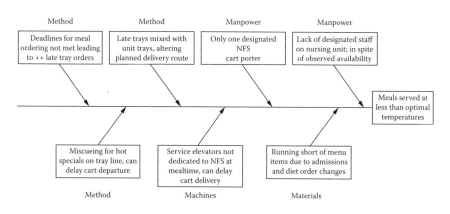

FIGURE 10.6
Fishbone cause-and-effects diagram, nutrition and food services, RDRHC.

Future State Map

The updated current map (Figure 10.7) is the proposed future state, including improvement opportunities based on the five material flow processes detailed in stage 1.

Using the Kaizen process, the Lean team studied the process observation forms, current map, and spaghetti diagrams to brainstorm on specific and practical solutions to enhance the flow of trays to and from the units. Our focus was to minimize non-value-added steps that delay the movement of trays at all process steps. We examined roles, responsibilities, and activities in the diet office and kitchen to see what the root causes of inefficiencies were and set improvement targets.

Production

- Can the hot catering list for short-order specials and add-ons beyond the established choice menu of the day be minimized?
- Are initial cooking activities set "just in time" for tray line startup?
- Are hot menu items cooked in batches and pulled as required to the tray line steam tables?
- Are recorded temperatures of hot menu items at the steam table pre- and post-tray line within an acceptable range?

Setup Tray Line

- Do all positions on the belt do a self-check that they are ready for assembly with all the necessary tools and food items in place?
- Could cutlery be pre-wrapped? What else could be preassembled?
- Are preheated alacite plates checked for warmth?
- Would a two-bin Kanban system for tray line supplies facilitate the establishment of a just-in-time inventory of required items?

Assemble and Load Trays

- Does the checker live by the goal that "the tray line must never stop"?
- Is there a better way to cue the cook for preparing hot short-order menu item specials?
- Are cloth cart covers adding non-value-added time to the process?

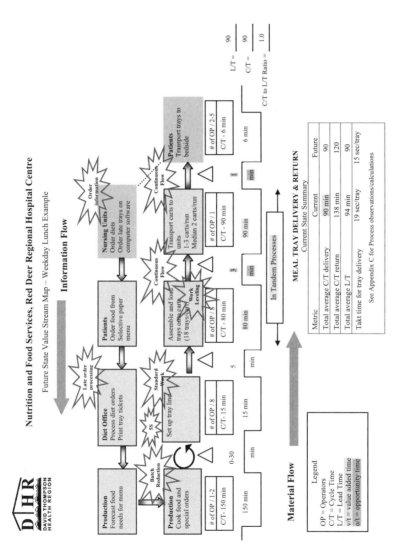

FIGURE 10.7

Future state map.

- Do the current insulated Aladdin bases and domes keep the food at a palatable temperature after plating and during transport?
- Should "late tray" assembly be separated from unit-by-unit assembly?
- What are the bottlenecks that stop the meal trays from flowing from the tray line to the cart to the unit to the patient?
- Could post-tray line audits be conducted to problem-solve on all events that delayed meal assembly?

Transport Carts to Units

- Are the twenty-five-year-old carts and cloth covers ready for retirement?
- Should late tray meal delivery be done separately from unit deliveries?
- Could carts be delivered one at a time without additional labor cost?
- Are the tugs a necessary tool for cart delivery?
- Should one of the service elevators be dedicated to NFS at mealtime?
- Do the units need an audiovisual signal when carts arrive at the unit?
- Do the current travel patterns for cart delivery make sense?

Transport Trays to Bedside

- Are carts difficult to maneuver and steer?
- Who decides which nursing unit staff helps with meal tray delivery?
- How and when do trays get reloaded on the carts after meal service?
- Should NFS and Nursing partner on meal tray audits to monitor food quality and temperature?

A series of three meetings with the Lean team led to the creation of a detailed project improvement matrix. The team agreed that implementing 5S on the tray line would improve organization and efficiencies to promote flow and prevent tray line stoppages. Based on the Lean principle of "getting it right the first time," it became clear that in terms of meal service, correct diet order entry from the nursing units is essential.

Value Stream Plan

The ideal state, as formally proposed on three occasions to senior administration, would be to renovate the tray line for cold meal assembly with meal rethermalization taking place on the units at a time selected by the unit in collaboration with the patients. The capital funding request to undertake such a major renovation has yet to be approved.

Process observations revealed that there appears to be sufficient nursing staff capacity to deliver and retrieve patient trays from the bedside. For a thirty-six-bed unit, five or six staff can easily distribute trays within six minutes. Our unexpected conclusion is that adding extra NFS staff to the process would not add value. In other words, the correct classification of staff to complete meal delivery is available. It is important that both NFS and Nursing be fully engaged in the process of patient meal service.

NFS needs to create and mobilize a shared commitment for meal delivery tasks with Nursing. As a starting point, joint audits of meal trays would provide ongoing feedback on how to improve our meal service with the emphasis on minimizing the timeframe from "pot to patient."

RESULTS AND LESSONS LEARNED

Our attitude and approach to process excellence must be based on the idea that we are working for the patient. In the ideal state, our patients would drive process improvements. Lean Thinking provides systematic ways to improve quality and make workforce improvements with our current processes and equipment.

We will undertake a number of projects to capture mapped improvement opportunities. All projects are in keeping with process flow, producing food closer to demand, and getting meal trays to the patient bedside at the most palatable temperature. Our focus on this goal will positively affect patient satisfaction scores and decrease turnaround times for tray leaving and returning to NFS. Ultimately, our prioritized improvement plans are in keeping with our NFS patient-driven mantra that "Good food is good medicine."

The staff selected to participate in this Kaizen event have responded positively to the use of Lean Thinking to solve our daily operational challenges. NFS has made an excellent start in defining project improvements and making action plans to work on process improvements. The Lean team will continue to work together and share improvement results with the entire department. The Lean Thinking journey has definitely begun, grounded in the belief that involvement leads to ownership, which leads to commitment, which leads to success.

Lean Team Details

The five-member team is a cross section of people from within the process being mapped: Shauna McGillicky, NFS manager; Sandra Schafer, NFS manager; Tammy Pearson, food service worker (meal tray cart delivery); Sylvia Holmes, floor aide (nourishment delivery); Judy-Ann Wybenga, senior regional manager; Lynn Lee, unit 22 unit manager; and Neda Kretschmer, regional director of NFS.

11

A Journey in Lean—Bringing about Change, Improving Quality for the Patient, and Developing the Culture of a Healthcare Organization

John Coleman and Tim Franklin

PROJECT BACKGROUND

This chapter is about an innovation in a National Health Service (NHS) acute trust in the West Midlands, U.K.—Good Hope Hospital at Sutton Coldfield. In autumn 2006, Good Hope was typical of many acute trusts in the United Kingdom. A hospital with some 500 beds and some 3,000 staff, Good Hope Hospital was grappling with complex of systems, multiple demands, targets, and limited resources.

So, like Chaucer's *Canterbury Tales*, this chapter charts not only the activities and process improvements, but also the personal journeys of a group of people—clinicians, managers, and nurses—who were instrumental in bringing about change, improving quality for the patient, and ultimately developing the culture of a leading U.K. NHS healthcare organization.

We acknowledge just some of the stakeholders in this project: Simon Dodds, Dr. Alastair Williamson, Liz Hamilton, Hanneke Huyskens, Caroline Mooney, Helen Pickard, Helen Charters, Jim Hearn, Dr. Hugh Raynor, Jo Chambers, Lyse Edwards, Lewis Deal, David Bowden, and the current board and senior management team at Heart of England Foundation Trust (HEFT).

Introducing Lean Thinking

Like most opportunities in life, a chance meeting played its part. We met with Simon Dodds in May 2006. Simon was running a seminar about improving patient quality through process redesign. This in itself seemed a curious activity for a vascular surgeon to undertake. But after some discussion with Simon, it was clear that he had been successfully applying elements of Lean in his work as a surgeon for some time. The conversations with Simon developed during the summer of 2006. This eventually led to us presenting to a cross section of the staff at Good Hope Hospital in the late summer.

It was at this point that the general manager in charge of surgery, Lyse Edwards, picked up the baton and championed the cause from a management and strategic perspective. Lyse was already familiar with the advantages of Lean in a healthcare setting. Also, with the awareness and benefits created by Simon's work, there was an increased motivation to apply Lean Thinking at Good Hope Hospital. We had already outlined our model of Lean skills transfer and support with the operational staff—the classic bottom-up approach. Simultaneously, managers such as Lyse, Lewis Grant, and the chief executive at this period, Jo Chambers, were applying the top-down support.

September 2006 saw the confirmation of the first pathway for Lean—the fractured neck of femur. In the outside world, the autumnal leaves may have been falling and nature was preparing to batten down for the winter; but inside Good Hope Hospital, new energy was stirring as the teams formed in readiness for Lean.

IMPLEMENTING LEAN

Fractured Neck of Femur

The staff at Good Hope had already identified that patients with a fractured neck of femur represented a vulnerable group. Usually they were elderly patients with a potentially complex mixture of social needs and medical conditions. A healthy outcome for the patient therefore required the concerted expertise of a large number of staff at Good Hope.

We had to have clear goals by which to judge success. At a stakeholder meeting, we created the overarching goals:

- Increase speed from the accident and emergency department (A&E) to the ward
- Increase admissions to trauma beds
- Increase speed from the ward to the theater
- Increase proportion of patients discharged home
- Improve outcome (reduce mortality rates)
- Improve bed utilization (reduce length of stay)
- Improve the staff and patient experience

The last objective was the most important; all the others were the contributing factors.

New Skills, New Knowledge

The model of Alturos is simple: we add new skills and knowledge to the excellence and wealth of technical competencies that *already* exist in any healthcare setting. The tools and techniques of Lean are valuable, but they are not the complete story and they do not guarantee success on their own. Other skills of change management are vital if Lean is to succeed.

A number of Good Hope staff, from all disciplines, "stepped up to plate" and volunteered to become change agents in Lean. Among those in the first wave were Dr. Alastair Williamson, a consultant anesthetist; Hanneke Huyskens, a nurse by training and a service improvement manager; Liz Hamilton, a nurse and midwife by training, who in 2006 was head of capacity. Simon Dodds and Lyse Edwards were also part of the champions team.

Value Stream Investigation

After developing new skills and knowledge, we then undertook the value stream investigation (VSI) in late September 2006. The value of the VSI should not be underestimated. It is more than brown paper, "sticky notes," and analysis of steps and data. The real value is to create agreement between all staff and a common understanding of the sheer complexity of patient pathways. In short, it is the start of the critical cultural change so often overlooked in Lean.

The home for the four-day VSI was a training and common room in the anesthetics department at Good Hope Hospital. It was near ward 15, the orthopedics ward, and also was central in the hospital. The area was large enough to accommodate the teams and also spacious enough for presenting the daily findings to a larger audience.

The VSI was started with tangible senior management support. Jo Chambers gave the opening presentation to the cross-functional team: orthopedic surgeons, orthopedic ward nurses, and staff; porters; change agents; managers and administrators; and IT and infomatics people. It was clear that this was not just "yet another change program."

Throughout the four days of the VSI, there were different responses and psychological reactions. This was a perfectly normal dynamic, and part of the process of accepting change. Some staff reached common agreement swiftly; others took more time. Indeed, there were often periods of heated debate.

What was clear early on in the VSI process was that the patient benefited from a rapid identification and confirmation of a fractured neck of femur and subsequent streaming to the right ward and trauma list. We also needed associated standard criteria for streaming the postoperative patients for rehabilitation and discharge. However, the further complexity of clinical issues and patient requirements, and therefore the correct streaming, took some time to resolve. A physician in elderly care, Dr. Helen Chamberlain, undertook some work in this area with her colleagues and created what was, in effect, a standardized work approach to this issue.

The evidence of the initial VSI mapping showed two very different and distinct dynamics of the fractured neck of femur pathway. The stream from A&E to preoperative to theater and then to postoperative patient stages was sequential and a "relatively well-behaved" function—but with clear areas for transformational redesign. However, the discharge section of the pathway was complex with different time scales, according to the discharge stream (Figure 11.1).

The team settled on improving the flow of patients from the A&E to the forty-eight-hour postoperative phase as the focus of the first rapid improvement activity (RIA).

The RIA team introduced the following major changes in the first phase:

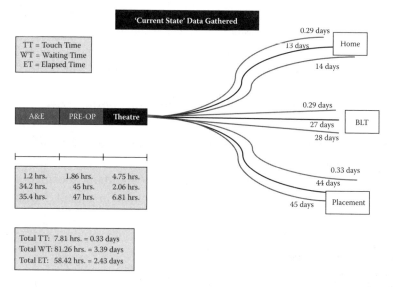

FIGURE 11.1
The current state of the fractured neck of femur pathway, from A&E to discharge. Courtesy of Hanneke Huyskens.

- A preallocated and protected fractured neck of femur slot on the daily trauma list for theaters
- A dedicated six-bed bay on the orthopedic ward for pre- and post-operative assessment and monitoring
- Standard work and agreed standard operating procedures within a multidisciplinary team for the dedicated area
- Pull systems that triggered vital activity such as radiology support

The Second Rapid Improvement Event—December 2006

The team reconvened in early December 2006 to start work on the discharge to the community (or home) element of the pathway. This involved other agencies, such as the PCT. At this point, Caroline Mooney, from the local Birmingham East and North Primary Care Trust, became involved. She said:

> This was a refreshing exercise. Two important parts of the healthcare system working together to speed up the patient discharge. It's about getting the patient experience and getting patient back to home, etc. The boundary

is an artificial one in reality. It's obvious now but the whole system has to work in unison. (Caroline Mooney, December 2006)

The RIA outcomes at this juncture were as follows:

- Clinical: Standard criteria for streaming postoperative patients through the pathway
- Information: Standard information hand-off between the various groups and stakeholders
- Information technology: The design of a standard information hub as a "pull" system to support the stakeholders in patient discharge

RESULTS AND LESSONS LEARNED

Early results were very promising. In an internal newsletter of December 2006 (Figure 11.2), the proportion of patients with fractured neck of femur now admitted to ward 15 was 83 percent (post-RIA), compared to 32 percent (pre-RIA). This early evidence appeared to confirm that the "pull" system of the assessment bay was working—there were fewer patient

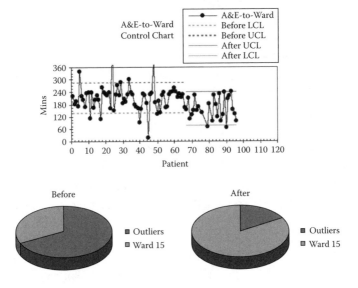

FIGURE 11.2
Early indications of success, December 2006. From the Good Hope Hospital newsletter.

outliers on other wards. In addition, there was an associated reduction (25 percent) in time taken to get from A&E to the assessment area. At this time, however, there was not enough data to assess the impact on length of stay.

The early, qualitative impact was also evident. There were fewer patient transfers, and doctors were not making unnecessary journeys to the outlier patients. Other factors were noted by the staff:

> I've seen other change activity before, but never with the speed and focus of this project. It's also refreshing that it is we, the staff, who are driving this, with the VSI and future state giving us solid evidence and direction for the change. (Nurse, ward 15)

Evaluation

Simon Dodds then undertook a detailed evaluation in September 2007, one year after the original VSI and subsequent redesign. Simon's assessment indicates that, as an illustrative run chart example, the patient admission time to assessment area did decrease because of the "pull" system of ward 15 (Figure 11.3). There was an increase in the "right first time" yield rate of the process, because more patients with fractured neck of femur were correctly routed to trauma beds. Also there was an

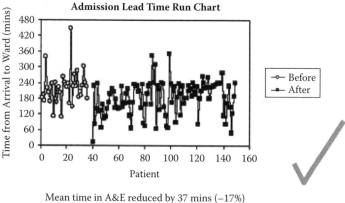

Mean time in A&E reduced by 37 mins (−17%)
Lead Time <4 hrs increased from 83% to 92%

FIGURE 11.3
Indicative evidence—a reduction in admission times to ward. Courtesy of Simon Dodds, Heart of England NHS Foundation Trust.

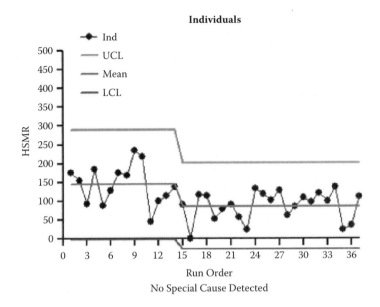

FIGURE 11.4
Indicative reduction in HSMR in the fractured neck of femur pathway. Courtesy of Simon Dodds, Heart of England NHS Foundation Trust.

associated reduction in outliers in nonorthopedic wards or blocking of elective orthopedic beds.

However, it was also clear that a very valuable, quality outcome was the reduction in mortality rates. Simon used Dr. Foster data from July 2005 to July 2008. There would appear to be a stable reduction in the average hospital standard mortality ratio (HSMR) that correlates with the fractured neck of femur work started in December 2006 (Figure 11.4).

Power of Communications during Lean

One of the many benefits of the VSI and subsequent RIAs at Good Hope was to broadcast, throughout the hospital, the patient and staff value of the Lean fractured neck of femur project. The teams were using e-mail and personal "persuasion" to entice colleagues to the briefing sessions.

But it was clear that there were more opportunities and channels of communications than e-mails. And so the road show was born. The team created a mobile storyboard, which was placed in the main corridor outside ward 15. Like a medieval market play, it certainly achieved its objective: staff and patients stopped and listened.

Simon Dodds was the "attention grabber" as he performed his juggling tricks; then the rest of the team would explain to the growing audience the activity and benefits of the project. Unusual? Yes, but it galvanized other staff and it certainly injected some much needed "serious" fun when energy levels were dropping. It also sent out a more subtle cultural message: here was a group of professionals (nurses, a surgeon, an anesthetist, and managers) all working on a focused, patient project, and traditional hierarchy and functional demarcations seemed to be suspended.

The senior management team at the time was also giving visible support and credibility to the project. During late autumn 2006, Jo Chambers had moved to a new post in another trust. David Bowden was then appointed to the position of managing and medical director at Good Hope Hospital. David picked up the baton in supporting Lean. He encouraged staff, through newsletters and personal conversations, to attend the feedback sessions and support Lean. He was also visible at many of the feedback sessions. Other internal newsletters were carrying the story. Local press coverage also took the story into the community served by Good Hope Hospital.

The power of clinical support and visible communications in Lean healthcare projects can never be underestimated. Clinicians, naturally, are a very influential group. At Good Hope Hospital, the foundation work of Simon Dodds meant that there was genuine interest from a wide group of clinicians in these early stages. As external consultants, we can sometimes find it a challenge to persuade clinicians that Lean is about getting patients to the value points of a healthcare system faster and smoothing out the flow. It is not about challenging their professionalism, but about bringing the clinical skills to the patient more rapidly and removing the layers of complexity. Many of the clinicians lead from the front at Good Hope Hospital. The support and practical involvement of Dr. Williamson, Simon Dodds, Liz Hamilton, and Hanneke Huyskens have already been mentioned. Another clinician was Dr. Paul Johnson, a colleague of Dr. Williamson in the anesthetics department at Good Hope Hospital. Dr. Johnson and Dr. Williamson led feedback sessions to large and influential groups during the fracture neck of femur project. Their overt support underscored and validated the process.

Where Next?

Like all journeys, there are respites and pauses to take stock, check the compass bearing, ... and then head off again. The heading off again came in February 2007 when Good Hope Hospital wanted to use Lean to focus on its acute respiratory patient pathway. The physician, Dr. Tim Fletcher, and ward sister, Anna Howell, had observed the fractured neck of femur project and were convinced that applying the same Lean principles would help their patients.

Spring 2007 saw another group of change agents being developed, ready for their Lean journey. Simon Dodds and Dr. Alastair Williamson were just as keen to support this new project. Interestingly, Liz Hamilton was taking a very active role in training staff and she worked alongside Alturos in this project. This was to be a turning point in Liz's career, as we shall see later.

After the acute respiratory pathway, it was evident that internal momentum for Lean was building and that more internal capacity was required. So we went on to develop more trainers in Lean at Good Hope Hospital. Liz Hamilton, Hanneke Huyskens, Caroline Mooney, and Anna Howell were the vanguard for the Alturos "Train the Trainer in Lean" project in May 2007.

During this period, Good Hope Hospital was also to be integrated with nearby Heartlands Hospital and Solihull Hospital to form the larger HEFT. This was to have another positive effect on the Lean activity at Good Hope, which is explained later.

The Tipping Point

In his book *Tipping Point*, Malcolm Gladwell (2000) describes how small things make a big difference and how "epidemics" can emerge from these small actions. Other scientists describe these phenomena in terms of nonlinear, complex adaptive systems, critical mass, or Lorenz's "butterfly effect." It really does not matter how we categorize them. What is important is that there appears to be a natural law that cannot be ignored. The next section describes that natural law at work in Good Hope Hospital and how Lean really took off.

Lean Academy

Good Hope Hospital was no exception to this seemingly natural law. During midsummer 2007, Alturos staff and Good Hope people were developing the next and by far the largest and most ambitious phase so far in their Lean journey. The feedback from patients and staff from the two previous projects was such that further pathways were being selected for Lean. At the same time, Liz Hamilton was moving more and more into a training role. She was already working with us in an informal role—but that role was about to be formalized as an internal Lean Academy was sanctioned by the HEFT senior management.

A Retrospective

It is tempting to use the well-known phrase from the Monty Python "Four Yorkshiremen" sketch that goes along the lines of "*...who would have thought it?*" But that phrase does sum up our view of the personal and organizational journey traveled by Good Hope Hospital staff in a little over two years. It was an intellectual and cultural journey of individuals and teams that has created many new organizational values.

In November 2008, the Good Hope Lean Academy moved to an even better home. It has new training rooms and dedicated areas for project development. It links with the other HEFT Lean Academies in joint projects. Alturos has worked with Liz in developing nearly 200 change agents and we have then gone on to support the teams with over eleven Lean pathway projects. These change agents have developed innumerable Lean projects of varying magnitude. Liz is now firmly established—along with manager Jim Hearn, Bruce Gray, and Ann Eason—in developing the next generation of Lean change agents. The next Lean journey step is not far way. We aim to use a goal deployment activity (what Alturos calls Pathfinder) to connect the dots and ensure that corporate objectives and Lean projects are linked.

In sum and substance: the Lean journey at Good Hope Hospital is a powerful example of what an innovative NHS trust can do. But Lean is simply a vehicle and means for change; it is not the end. It is the motivation of caring individuals, sound local and corporate leadership, and cultural change that are the vital ingredients.

ACKNOWLEDGMENTS

Simon Dodds for his evaluation data and the contributions by other Good Hope Staff. Contributions from Liz Hamilton, Dr. Alastair Williamson, and other members of Good Hope Hospital staff are also gratefully acknowledged. Photographs: All photographs, unless otherwise stated, are the copyright of John Coleman and Tim Franklin.

12

Process Improvements to Reduce Operating Room Cancellations

Mimi Kokoska, Samuel B. Welch, and Teresa Stevens
Central Arkansas Veterans Healthcare System, Little Rock, Arkansas

PROJECT BACKGROUND

Project Goal

The goal of the Lean operating room (OR) cancellation workgroup was to reduce OR cancellations at the Central Arkansas Veterans Healthcare System (CAVHS). The term "OR cancellation" refers to cancellation of a scheduled surgical patient.

Project Selection

The surgical services at CAVHS comprise multiple surgical specialties including cardiac, general (GS), neurosurgery, eye, dental, orthopedic (ortho), otolaryngology–head and neck surgery (ENT), peripheral vascular (PV), plastic, podiatry (POD), thoracic surgery (TS), and urology. OR cancellation rates varied significantly between subspecialties. The preoperative processing and preparation of surgical patients differ between the subspecialties, partly because of the distinct differences in clinical requirements. For example, bowel preparation is frequently required in GS patients, whereas different preoperative preparation may be necessary in POD or ortho patients. Therefore, we anticipated that although there would likely be components of the preoperative process and preparation that are ubiquitous for all surgical patients, it would be best to focus on a particular subspecialty. This would enable us to conduct a thorough examination with specific recommendations for a particular area. Of course, if improvements were identified that were applicable to other or all subspecialties, we planned to recommend implementing them service-wide.

Rationale for Project Selection

The area initially chosen for improvement was GS, because a review of the data indicated that this was the subspecialty with the greatest number of cancellations (84 of 528; Table 12.1); in other words, GS had a 16 percent cancellation rate from October 2007 through January 2008. Its impact value (as calculated by cancellation rate multiplied by the total volume) was the highest for all the surgical specialties.

However, after the endoscopy component was excluded from GS, we found that the GS OR cancellation rate was 11 percent (31 cancellations of 291 total cases; Table 12.1). The endoscopy OR cancellation rate was 22 percent (53 cancellations of 237 total cases). Because endoscopy was already being evaluated through the chief of staff office for process improvement, we decided it would be redundant for the Lean OR cancellation workgroup to focus on endoscopy. After factoring out endoscopy from GS, we reevaluated the data to see which surgical area had the greatest cancellation impact factor (highest cancellations and patient volume).

During this same time period from October 07 to January 08, orthopedic surgery had a cancellation rate of 14 percent (53 cancellations out of 374 total cases). Although thoracic surgery had a higher cancellation rate at 27 percent, the impact value (0.27×33 total cases) was less than that for orthopedic surgery (0.14×374 total cases). In addition to having the highest impact value, anesthesia and ambulatory surgery representatives agreed that OR cancellations in orthopedic surgery occurred frequently, which resulted in significant problems in OR utilization. Therefore, we decided to direct our efforts at improving orthopedic surgery OR cancellations.

Importance of Project to the Veterans Health Administration (VHA) and CAVHS

The six VHA value domains are quality, access, satisfaction, functional status, community health, and cost effectiveness. The leadership and facilities are measured by how they perform in these domains. The Lean OR

TABLE 12.1

Surgery Cancellations in FY08 (FY08 Surgery Cancellations through 1-31-08)

Reason (see below)	A	B	C	D	E	F	G	H	I	J	K	L	M	Total Cancellations -FY08 to Date
Anes change in staff opinion							1							1
Anes needs further workup		1	1		1	1	3							7
OR instruments not available			1				2							3
OR lack of staff			1	1			1							3
OR lack of time		1	1				2				1			5
Pt abnl coagulation times	2	1					2							5
Pt abnl lab values	1				1		3	1				2	1	9
Pt abnl lab values other					1									1
Pt change condition/sick		1	18		10	1	8	3	3			1	4	49
Pt changed their mind			18		1	1	3	2					3	28
Pt drug screen positive			1	2		1	1		1					6
Pt family emergency								1			1			2
Pt no show	1		26	1	1		2	2	1		1		1	36
Pt no show to preop visit					2									2
Pt not NPO			2		2		3						1	8
Pt site compromised			1				8							9

(continued on next page)

TABLE 12.1 (continued)

Surgery Cancellations in FY08 (FY08 Surgery Cancellations through 1-31-08)

Reason (see below)	A	B	C	D	E	F	G	H	I	J	K	L	M	Total Cancellations -FY08 to Date
Pt transportation			1				1	1						3
Pt weather			1											1
Surgeon change staff opinion			1									1		2
Surgeon emergency supersedes	1		1	1			2						4	9
Surgeon error in scheduling	2		6				1		4		1			14
Surgeon lack of staff	2	1			2		2			1	1	1	2	12
Surgeon needs further work up		3	3	1	2		4	2	2		1	4		22
Surgeon prosthesis not avail							1							1
Surgeon surgery not indicated			1		1		3	1	2	1			1	10
Total cancellations FY08 to date	9	8	84	6	24	4	53	13	13	2	6	9	17	248
Total scheduled cases FY08 to date	67	46	528	74	352	15	374	125	109	13	32	33	195	1972
% Cancellations by specialty	13%	17%	16%	8%	7%	27%	14%	10%	12%	15%	19%	27%	9%	13%

Cancellation reasons: A, cardiac; B, card; C, GS; D, neuro; E, eye care; F, dental; G, ortho; H, ENT; I, PV; J, plastic; K, Pod; L, TS; M, urology.

Data Source: V16 Data Warehouse as of 1/31/08.

cancellation project is important to VHA and its stakeholders because it affects all these domains. In addition, OR cancellations are a part of the VHA FIX initiative, which is a national inpatient flow improvement initiative. This underscores the importance VHA has placed on OR cancellations.

Anticipated Improvements from Project

We predict that with the implementation of Lean in this project there will be reduced human effort, reduced need for operational space, decreased capital investment, fewer wasted materials and services, and increased patient throughput. As a result of these improvements and goal-oriented teamwork throughout the project, we expect greater customer and employee satisfaction.

There will be less human effort because there will be fewer cancellations to process. If a patient is canceled in Ambulatory Surgery right before he or she is supposed to be taken into the OR, there is a good chance the following processes have occurred: (1) intravenous line and fluids already hung and will need to be removed; (2) the OR informed consent process completed and form signed; (3) the OR nursing and technical staff likely already set up the OR for the case; (4) a completed preoperative surgical history and physical examination; (5) a completed anesthesia preoperative assessment and note; and (6) if the patient does not end up completing the surgery within thirty days of the completed blood work or informed consent, the patient would need to have the lab work repeated and reconsented for the procedure if it is rescheduled. All these human efforts become wasted when surgery is canceled.

A reduction in OR cancellations would improve the utilization of ambulatory surgery space, operating rooms, and operating room personnel. This will also reduce or defer the need for additional operating rooms. The cost to build one operating room is approximately $1.6 million.

At CAVHS, a patient is defined as "scheduled for surgery" if the patient appears on the final surgical schedule at 2:00 p.m. the day before the surgery date. The patient is defined as "canceled" if he or she is removed from the surgery schedule any time after 2:00 p.m. the day before the surgery date. If a patient is canceled from the operating room schedule, this results in underutilization of ambulatory surgery beds and ORs. Essentially, in most canceled cases, there is not enough time to replace the abandoned spot with another outpatient case.

────────

IMPLEMENTING LEAN

Approach and Initial Planning

Roles and Contributions of Team Members

Mimi Kokoska was group leader from workgroup inception through July 2008. She has continued to monitor and analyze processes and provided guidance to the group into September 2008. Her contributions included setting agendas for the meetings and helping to define the goal of the workgroup. She also provided a Lean overview to the workgroup, because most members were not knowledgeable about Lean initially. She drew the current state map of the OR scheduling and preoperative process and she subsequently led a subgroup in reviewing sixty-nine medical records. Dr. Kokoska also led the workgroup in determining which interventions would provide the most positive impact in the three categories. She then monitored and followed up with individuals to verify the processes were in place.

Samuel Welch was group leader from August 2008 through September 2008. He provided valuable guidance to workgroup discussions. He also helped to refine the surgery history and physical template to include patient telephone contact so the preoperative telephone calls could be completed through a recently updated telephone number.

Teresa Stevens extracted the OR cancellation data, which allowed the workgroup to analyze the reasons for cancellation. She assisted with reviewing the sixty-nine medical records and modifying the reasons for cancellation accordingly. She also collected and tallied patient check-off lists on a weekly basis, beginning in July. She provided the workgroup with the monthly outcomes report from July through December 2008.

Other contributing team members included Steven Lee, Leslie Gayle Wildhagen, David Paladino, Nell Jackson, Anne Mancino, Kathy Thornton, Annette Prieur, and Theodora Terlea.

Team Communications

The Lean OR cancellations workgroup initially had two members who were familiar with Lean management concepts. These two individuals (Dr. Kokoska and Dr. Welch) were members of the Lean steering committee, and they voluntarily committed to the Lean OR cancellations workgroup. Before the first meeting, Dr. Kokoska contacted the rest of the workgroup members individually to personally review the goals of the workgroup and to ensure the members were interested in actively contributing to the workgroup. A written statement of the group goals with an agenda outline for the first meeting was e-mailed to the entire workgroup. The first meeting began with a brief Microsoft PowerPoint presentation about Lean Thinking. Then the group developed the preoperative scheduling current state map.

Between the twice-a-month workgroup meetings, e-mails were frequently used to communicate within subgroups and external CAVHS staff who were recruited to assist with specific efforts or process modifications. In addition, subgroups had impromptu conversations or meetings with Dr. Kokoska to vet questions, concerns, or ideas between workgroup meetings. These interim meetings allowed the group to modify the processes immediately, instead of having to wait weeks for the next meeting. This helped to expedite the implementations and allowed the group to start the interventions in early June. Since the preoperative processing usually occurs within thirty days prior to the scheduled surgery date, it was clear that the outcomes of any intervention would not be evident until approximately one month later.

Lean Tools and Practices

The group aimed to achieve the five core goals associated with Lean Thinking: (1) identify and enhance process value streams; (2) track and reduce waste; (3) modify process flow in order to reduce OR cancellations; (4) aim for continuous improvement and perfection; and (5) work toward achieving seamless integration with all parties in the process.

The group believed that the best strategy to utilize Lean effectively was first to develop a current state map and process flow diagram. In doing so, it became clear that timed studies were not going to help achieve a reduction in OR cancellations because the goal was to reduce OR cancellations, and not to decrease cycle times. The OR cancellation rate during the preceding period (07/1/07 to 12/31/07; Table 12.2), was used as the baseline reference for OR cancellation data and for comparison with subsequent post-intervention results. The group used standardization of work to optimize the preoperative counseling and education process and surgery

TABLE 12.2

Orthopedic Surgery Cancels FY08 (through 3/31/08)

Patient Cancellations	Pt status		
Cancel Reason	IP	OP	Grand Total
Anes change in staff opinion		1	1
Anes needs further workup or not seen in preop	2	7	9
Emergency case supersedes		1	1
Lab drug screen positive		2	2
OR instruments not available	1	1	2
OR lack of staff	1	1	2
OR lack of time		2	2
Pt abnl coagulation times	1	2	3
Pt abnl lab values		2	2
Pt change condition/sick	3	6	9
Pt changed their mind	2	2	4
Pt no show		4	4
Pt not NPO		5	5
Pt site compromised	1	13	14
Pt transportation		2	2
Surgeon lack of staff	1		1
Surgeon prosthesis not avail		2	2
Surgeon surgery not indicated	1	2	3
Grand total	13	55	68

Data Source: V16 DW as of 3/31/08.

confirmation process. In addition, 5S was used throughout the period first to initiate the review, then to improve the processes, and finally to ensure continuous improvement and compliance.

The following Lean tools and practices were used to improve process flow.

1. Process Flow Diagram

   Process flow diagram (PFD) enabled ortho to change its processes from a push to pull system. The group developed a current state map of the preoperative processing of orthopedic surgery patients. This enabled us to walk through the service as a user from beginning to end, and develop a visual map of the information flow and materials exchanged during the entire process. It provided a means for identifying non-value-added steps or activities and a visual understanding of the unique aspects of medical and scheduling needs of orthopedic patients. We could then determine the interventions that would address the principal reasons for cancellations while not requiring additional human resources, OR rooms, or capital.

2. Standardized Work

We used standardized work to optimize the activities of the orthopedic advance practice nurses (APNs) and PAs, the ambulatory surgery preoperative telephone communications, and the documentation used in the preoperative process. The preoperative telephone call from an ambulatory surgery nurse to a scheduled surgery patient normally occurs on the day before surgery (after 2:00 p.m. on the day prior to scheduled surgery). Because any scheduled surgeries that are removed from the schedule after 2:00 p.m. on the day prior to surgery are deemed cancellations, any patient who decided to not proceed with next day's surgery or was identified as suboptimal for surgery (because of anticoagulation, for example) during the preoperative telephone call was subsequently removed from the schedule and was already by default an OR cancellation.

One Lean intervention was to move the preoperative telephone call to two to three business days before the scheduled date of orthopedic surgery. The ambulatory surgery preoperative nurses also noted that in many cases they could not reach the patient to communicate the preoperative instructions and confirmation because they could not identify a correct patient telephone number in the medical record. Many times, the telephone number that was listed on the patient information page of the electronic record was incorrect.

A second Lean intervention was to insert a current telephone prompt in the surgery preoperative history and physical template, which is completed when the patient is initially scheduled or seen for surgery. This template is used throughout the entire surgical services, so this improvement would help all surgical subspecialties. The ambulatory surgery nurses now had a place to locate a current contact number quickly.

The ambulatory surgery nurses used a general telephone call template for all surgical services. The template reminded the patient to avoid eating or drinking and a few other general instructions. A Lean intervention was to standardize the preoperative telephone call template for orthopedic surgery patients to ensure these preoperative instructions were consistent with the preoperative education they received from the orthopedic staff. Through discussions with the ambulatory surgery nurses, the preoperative telephone template was tailored to ensure consistency and reinforce the instructions previously provided by the ortho APNs and PA.

These standardized templates helped to decrease variation and inconsistency and, therefore, increase quality levels in the steps and tasks within the preoperative process. It also helped to ensure higher levels of safety because anesthesia and ortho guidelines were incorporated into the standardized work. The quality of patient communications improved by increasing the meaningfulness of the standardized content in the templates.

3. 5S

We applied 5S, the five-level standard for organizing the ortho pre-operative work environment. First, we used 1S (Sort) to eliminate unnecessary information in the preoperative educational materials. Then we used 2S (Set in order) to organize the interventions to ensure the majority of reasons for cancellations were addressed. All services or individuals who had an impact on these areas were included in the process improvement. This was followed by 3S (Shine), in which we tested the templates for a few weeks and modified them to eliminate unclear or unnecessary text. We used 4S (Standardize) to increase consistency in all the preoperative counseling, education, and pre-operative telephone call information. Throughout the process, we applied 5S (Sustain) to maintain an environment of continued compliance. This was accomplished by continually analyzing ongoing data and reporting the results to the group, while modifying templates or processes as needed and acknowledging ongoing contributions and achievements by individuals and the workgroup.

Steps to Enlist Stakeholder Support

The Lean OR cancellation workgroup members were provided with an overview of Lean principles. The goal of the workgroup was outlined at the first meeting. The additional stakeholders who would be affected by the changes were informed about the goals and modifications being considered by the workgroup. The chief of orthopedic surgery was informed of the goal of the Lean OR cancellation workgroup, and permission was obtained to include the ortho APNs and PA in the workgroup. Because the

APNs and PA perform most of the preoperative counseling and coordination, it was critical not only to have their support, but also to have their input into the analysis and interventions.

In addition, the ambulatory surgery preoperative nurses, the anesthesia scheduler, an anesthesiologist, and the nurse on duty participated. The group worked directly with these individuals to obtain input regarding modifications or interventions.

Positive reinforcement or credits were given to individuals who provided noteworthy efforts during group meetings or via group e-mails. In addition, the supervisors of these individuals were informed in writing of the individual's significant contributions. The progress and interim results were provided to all key individuals.

Current Situation

We decided to use the OR cancellation rates for the same months in the previous year as those months evaluated in our post-intervention assessment period. This would eliminate seasonal variability in OR usage and cancellations. Therefore, we compared the results for the six-month period to 12/31/07 with the corresponding period for 2008. The current state map of the ortho preoperative process enabled us to define the current steps in scheduling and preparing a patient for surgery.

The pre-Lean preoperative counseling and education processes were not specifically designed to prevent the common causes for OR cancellations. For example, a review of sixty-nine cancelled OR cases, including inpatient (IP) and outpatients (OP), found there were causes of "pt not NPO," because patients did not know which activities to avoid, such as chewing gum and chewing tobacco (considered by anesthesia as oral intake).

Diagnostic Work to Improve Understanding of Current Situation

Once we identified the major reasons for ortho OR cancellations during the review period (Table 12.2), it became clear that many of the OR cancels were patient-controllable factors. For example, one factor was "Pt Site Compromised," where the operative skin site has a rash or other skin abnormality identified just before surgery; this results in a cancellation. Orthopedic surgeons do not operate through areas with skin pathology because of the higher risk for implant or wound infections. Because so many of the reasons for cancellations were patient-controllable factors, we decided to use preoperative instruction and education to better instruct patients on preparation for surgery. The patients were instructed to report any abnormalities in advance of the 2:00 p.m. day-before deadline.

We conducted numerous analyses of the data to identify patterns and to determine the most pressing areas for improvement. For example, in this analysis, contrary to our intuitive thinking, those patients who resided close by (60 miles or fewer) accounted for more of the cancellations than those who lived far away (120 miles or more). Perhaps those patients who lived far away actually made a greater preparatory investment into their planned surgery, because transportation and lodging are greater concerns for them.

We also examined surgeon-specific data to see whether there were patterns associated with certain surgeons. As a result, we found that the hand and oncology patients had the highest number of cancellations. The group decided to ensure that all the ortho APNs and PA had templates that addressed the specific needs of their patients. For example, we decided to include "Anesthesia needs further work up or not seen in pre-op" as a reason for cancellation because it was a significant factor.

Defining the Future and Achieving Improvements

We used the data and chart reviews to identify the areas for improvement. And we addressed the major reasons for cancellations. We developed an ortho preoperative instruction check-off sheet (Figure 12.1). We also designed a similar ortho preoperative instruction check-off sheet (Figure 12.2) specifically for hand surgery patients.

We reviewed the average ortho OR surgery case times to determine the approximate financial implications of OR cancellations.

We determined that the nurse on duty (NOD) was the best available person after hours to answer logistical questions from scheduled surgery patients because this alternating administrative nurse was in-house. The final surgery schedule was displayed in the NOD's office and we developed a NOD template (Figure 12.3) as another example of standardization of work.

In addition, the ambulatory surgery preoperative telephone call (Figure 12.4) now occurs two or three business days before the ortho scheduled surgery. The template standardizes the instructions that are

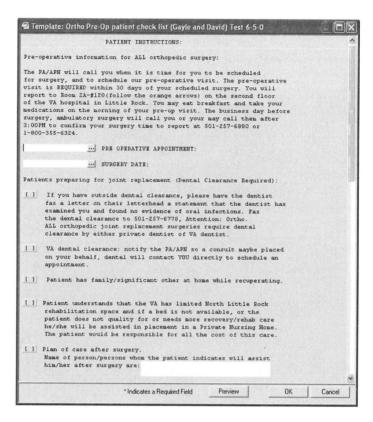

FIGURE 12.1
Ortho preoperative instruction check-off sheet.

provided to patients, with ample time to remove a patient from the schedule prior to the 2:00 p.m. cancellation deadline.

RESULTS AND LESSONS LEARNED

The ortho OR cancellation rate has been reduced from 14 to 8 percent (Table 12.3). During the review period, the volume of scheduled orthopedic surgery cases was lowest in December. Seasonal or temporal patterns (vacations, hunting seasons, holidays, and so on) influence patient behavior. This highlights the importance of comparing the outcomes with the same monthly period from the previous year.

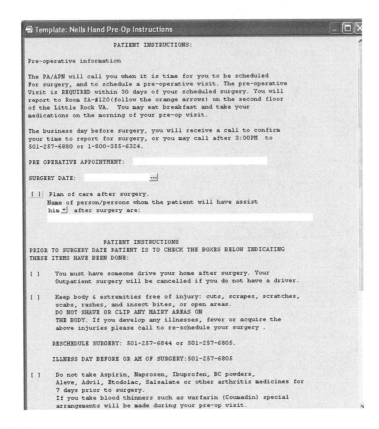

FIGURE 12.2
Ortho preoperative instruction check-off sheet for hand surgery.

There was more variability in the first three months following the initial Lean implementation. The first month result prompted a review of how each Lean intervention was being followed by the front line. We discovered that one key ortho nurse practitioner had not been informed of the new preoperative and patient education template, which was subsequently modified to address the subspecialty-specific patients that she oversees. Therefore, two ortho preoperative and patient education templates were ultimately developed as part of this process to address the specific needs of patients with needs ranging from total hip replacement to hand surgery. The outcomes from a modification are not reflected in the immediate month following the change. There was less variability in the outcomes from October to December 2008, which supports the theory that the initial irregularities were suitably resolved. These results highlight the

---

INSTRUCTIONS FOR AFTER-HOURS PHONE CALLS REGARDING NEXT DAY SURGERY

1. NOD will refer to the daily surgery schedule printout (out after 2:00 p.m., printed to printer# PT62034).
2. Patient should be told to arrive in Ambulatory Surgery 1.5 hours prior to the scheduled OR time on the printout.
3. If a patient states he/she is scheduled for next-day surgery, but the name is not on the printed schedule, he/she may be an add-on. Add-ons may not appear on the schedule if they were added on after 2:00 p.m. the day before. Therefore, patients who are not on the printed schedule, but state they are having surgery the next day but they do not know when to arrive, should be told to remain NPO after midnight and to call Ambulatory Surgery in the morning (next working day at 6:30 a.m.) to find out when they are to arrive for surgery. Please DO NOT tell these patients that they are not having surgery the next day since they could very well be an add-on.

FIGURE 12.3
NOD template.

importance of monitoring the initial results, as they are indicators of implementation success.

During implementation, patients were asked to return their check-off sheets to see whether using check-off sheets influenced the overall cancellation rate. Of the 206 total scheduled surgeries in July and August 2008, 63 check-off sheets were returned. Therefore, it does not appear that returning the check-off sheets significantly influenced the cancellation rate.

A previous study suggests that OR cancellations result in a loss of between $1,400 and $1,700 per hour, plus hospital-variable costs.[1] When these figures are applied to the orthopedic cancellations, the costs associated with the 86 orthopedic surgery cancellations in July to December 2007 can be conservatively estimated at $1,565 per hour—using the median of $1,565 loss per hour and three hours of surgery ($1,565 × 3 hours = $ lost per canceled ortho case × 86 canceled cases = $403K). Therefore, in one year, ortho cancellations alone could cost a minimum of $800K. The estimated impact cost of $800K, does not include the labor and materials costs spent in processes that prepare a patient for the operating room, which were mentioned earlier. Clearly, all OR cancellations across surgical services cost the organization millions of dollars annually per VA facility.

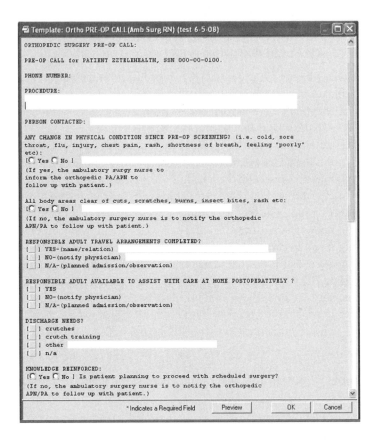

FIGURE 12.4

Ambulatory surgery preoperative telephone call template.

TABLE 12.3

Ortho Pre-Lean and Post-Lean Monthly Cancellation Comparison

Monthly Cancel Rate—Pre- and Post-Lean Implementation	Pre-Lean-(Jul 07–Dec 07)			Post-Lean- (Jul 08–Dec 08)		
	Cancels	Scheduled Surg	Cancel Rate	Cancels	Scheduled Surg	Cancel Rate
July	14	114	12%	12	103	12%
August	22	142	15%	7	103	7%
September	8	81	10%	14	106	13%
October	15	124	12%	4	112	4%
November	21	104	20%	6	73	8%
December	6	72	8%	5	79	6%
Grand total	**86**	**637**	**14%**	**48**	**576**	**8%**

Modifications to the Original Plan

Changing the focus from general surgery to ortho enabled the group to make a significant impact by selecting a high-impact surgical specialty.

The return of check-off sheets did not appear to influence whether the patient was ultimately canceled. It was a surprise that this specific reinforcing act did not result in a noticeable difference.

We learned that Lean can be tailored to deal with specific problem areas. Healthcare is a fertile arena to apply Lean because its processes are complicated. Lean tools helped to guide how we could ensure compliance with documentation needs and patient education challenges.

Lean as a Journey

We identified and modified a number of processes during the orthopedic surgery review. This included templates that can be used across all surgical services (for example, a specific check-off sheet for the preoperative ambulatory surgery telephone call) or that can be easily tailored for use by each surgical subspecialty (for example, a preoperative patient check-off sheet). Because Dr. Welch had been involved with the Lean workgroup, he had the tools to drive continuous improvement in OR cancellations for all surgical subspecialties and apply Lean to other areas within surgical services and the facility, and in the future. Therefore, he was passed the baton of leading the Lean OR cancellation workgroup when Dr. Kokoska relocated, although she maintained surveillance of the project. A Lean champion should be identified for a project and is perhaps even more critical when there are transitions in leadership during the process improvement period.

5S has been and will continue to be used to achieve and maintain continuous improvement toward reaching perfection. Since implementing improvements, outcome metrics have been used to monitor and assess the ortho OR cancellation rate to ensure that consistency has been maintained. The monthly data obtained will be continually used to modify processes or flow to fuel further improvements.

ACKNOWLEDGMENTS

The authors acknowledge the other contributing Lean OR cancellations team members including Steven Lee, Leslie Gayle Wildhagen, David Paladino, Nell Jackson, Anne Mancino, Kathy Thornton, Annette Prieur, and Theodora Terlea for their input and service.

REFERENCE

1. Dexter, F., E. Marcon, R. H. Epstein, and J. Ledolter. 2005. Validation of statistical methods to compare cancellation rates on the day of surgery. *Anesth Analg* 101: 465–73.

13

The Future for Lean Healthcare

Timothy D. Hill

ROOTS OF LEAN

Lean management is not a new concept. My own research in the early 1980s showed a "Lean" connection between Toyoda and others that goes back to their roots in textiles. Toyoda is the family name behind Toyota, the car company, and elements of the world-renowned Toyota Production System (TPS) go back to the late 1800s and the family's textile business. Relatively speaking, Lean is new to healthcare.

Drawn from TPS and called Lean by the authors of *The Machine That Changed the World,* Lean/TPS refers to sustainable Lean, as developed and practiced by Toyota since 1949.

The roots of Lean are certainly deep, and they have spread to a wide range of areas, most notably in the manufacturing and automotive sectors. In many ways, healthcare is where manufacturing was about thirty years ago. Manufacturing suffered from poor process practices, poor cycle time, long waiting periods, very high error rates, and more. Right now, healthcare shares all these symptoms.

I have heard healthcare people say their sector is so complex that car company best practices have no place in their world. I have heard them say medical professionals will refuse standard work and even threaten to strike if standard work was enforced. Although they are right when they say that patients are not cars, they are very wrong when they say their processes are inordinately complex, more complex than simple car company "best practices" could cope with.

Healthcare leaders who have been early Lean adopters have seen the light—any process can be improved, and healthcare has processes. Because the roots of Leans are concerned with increasing the flow through any process while making the entirety of that process more visible, they saw the attraction of Lean.

Early Lean healthcare leaders include the following:

- Virginia Mason in the United States
- ThedaCare in the United States
- Flinders Medical Centre in Australia
- The National Health Service in the United Kingdom

Leaders of these organizations also emphasized the importance of creating a sustainable Lean work culture that is ready and willing to accept new thinking and best practices. Given the 80:20 balance of culture versus tools, the failure to build the culture means that Lean/TPS will fail.

As much as new books about Toyota and Lean try to present the "secrets" of this "new" quality system, much of Lean is based on the work of W. Edwards Deming. He emphasized that that managers should get out of their offices and focus on improving processes in order to increase flow of work and build quality into the product.

Lean is not a cost-reduction program. It is a management practice applicable to all organizations because it improves processes. All organizations—including healthcare organizations—are composed of a series of processes intended to create value for those who use or depend on them (customers or patients). Process improvement is driven by business practices supported by site leadership. The Toyota business practices are arguably the world's best and have been successful for more than a century.

TOYOTA'S BUSINESS PRACTICES

Toyota's business practices have followed an eight-step plan:

1. Clarify the problem so that everyone knows about the problem. This includes going to the site of the problem to see firsthand.
2. Break down the problem so that the elements are clear.

3. Target specific problems within the larger problem; set and rank them from largest to smallest.

4. Perform a root-cause analysis to ask the right question about which problem to address and how.

5. Develop a solution (countermeasure) and set a specific goal for success. Typically, the goal is to reduce the problem to zero. Creating overhead to manage a problem is not acceptable.

6. With the countermeasure and objectives ready, implement the solution.

7. Don't assume that the "fix has gone to plan." Monitor results and processes.

8. When the change is stabilized, standardize the change by refining the processes to reflect the countermeasures and improvements.

Books such as *Extreme Toyota* get attention because Toyota emphasizes continuous change and improvement while requiring standard work. This often confuses people. To get "reliable and stable change," Toyota requires an improvement to standard work. This Kaizen approach (Figure 13.1) improves the standard and then the standard becomes the stable process.

By building many small steps for improvement, Toyota avoids two mistakes. It will not fall backward after change. And it will not lose competitive advantage by waiting for big changes—running the risk of missing market and customer influences.

Lean Thinking drives everyone's involvement in increasing the flow of work to build a just-in-time practice (Figure 13.2). The other element is

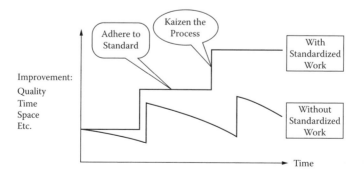

FIGURE 13.1
Using Kaizen with standard work.

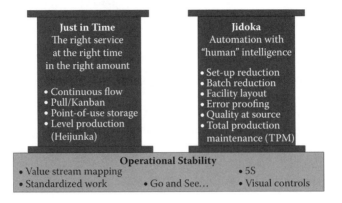

FIGURE 13.2

Just in time (JIT) and Jidoka.

Jidoka, the practice of making things visible so that problems are no longer hidden and can be eliminated.

GLOBAL CRISIS IN HEALTHCARE

It's fair to say that all the healthcare leaders who were early Lean adopters were driven by some manner of crisis. For example, the Flinders Medical Centre (FMC) was constantly in the newspapers in 2003 because of overcrowding in the emergency room (ER), delays in treatments, ambulance diversions, clinical outcomes being compromised, and other problems. Internal and external Emergency Department (ED) safety reviews were uniformly critical. The center was at the breaking point.

The problems at FMC are worldwide and more healthcare money is not the answer. The United States leads the world in per-person healthcare costs but delivers some of the world's worst healthcare. In the United States, increased spending on Medicare and Medicaid reflects the fact that it has an aging population with greater problems, and increased insurance and delivery costs.

My country, Canada, is not that far behind. More money is not the answer to the healthcare crisis, even though it is typically the first thing that non-Lean healthcare leaders call for. The U.S. and Canadian examples apply worldwide. The Boomer generation's increases in behavioral pathogens act as a multiplier for all that is wrong in healthcare.

Healthcare Crisis: Behavioral Pathogens

The U.S. Centers for Disease Control (CDC) Behavioral Risk Factor Surveillance System reports behavioral pathogen data. BRFSS data from three years (1990, 1998 and 2007). The growth rate for the highest level of obesity is increasing dramatically. In addition to the adult population increases, there is data that the obesity rates for the youth population are growing even faster.

Consequences of Obesity

Research has shown that as weight increases to reach the levels referred to as "overweight" and "obese," the risks for the following conditions also increase:[1]

- Coronary heart disease
- Type 2 diabetes
- Cancers (endometrial, breast, and colon)
- Hypertension (high blood pressure)
- Dyslipidemia (for example, high total cholesterol or high levels of triglycerides)
- Stroke
- Liver and gallbladder disease
- Sleep apnea and respiratory problems
- Osteoarthritis (a degeneration of cartilage and its underlying bone within a joint)
- Gynecological problems (such as abnormal menses or infertility)

Healthcare Errors

Errors are becoming more costly for hospitals. Patients and their loved ones have long felt the effects of the patient safety and quality problems in the industry.

The Institute of Medicine estimates that nearly 100,000 patients die in hospitals each year because of medical errors, with more than half of these errors preventable. This is three times the number of people who die on highways. It does not include deaths that occur in ambulatory settings or deaths after discharge that resulted from medical errors when the patient was hospitalized.[2]

The *New England Journal of Medicine* reported in 2003 that the quality of adult healthcare in the United States was startlingly poor. In that study, 439 indicators of clinical quality of care were reviewed from the medical records of 6,712 patients, for thirty acute and chronic conditions, plus prevention. Participants received about half of the prescribed care. The conclusion: the "defect rate" in the technical quality of American healthcare was about 45 to 50 percent.

Lean has been used to tackle hand-washing and hospital-borne infections. The Canadian Broadcasting Corporation (CBC) reported that every year, 250,000 Canadians pick up infections while they are in hospitals being treated for something else. That's a staggering one of every nine Canadians who are admitted to the hospital becoming infected while the prevention was blazingly simple. Every year, those infections kill more than 8,000 people.

LEAN IN HEALTHCARE

One of my mentors, Dr. W. Edwards Deming, wrote almost twenty years ago that one of the world's worst exports was a management style that focused on short-term gains and not long-term improvement. During the 1980s and 1990s, healthcare started to adopt cost cutting, shared costs to reduce overhead, and more, but it was still largely a U.S.-style management philosophy—create HMOs to drive economy of scale; see more patients per day; have direct billing to patients and insurers; reduce wait times for payments and more. All had their part in creating the healthcare crisis while demand skyrocketed.

Canada is catching up to Lean, with leaders calling for Lean as the medicine for healthcare. The Quebec health minister has turned to Toyota for inspiration, saying the Toyota way is a "common sense approach to improving quality."[3]

The Health Council of Canada (HCC) was created to monitor how money for healthcare is being spent. HCC reported that the "state of healthcare reform in Canada today is largely a patchwork of pilot projects, not a model of system-wide change." In a report this year, it listed nine areas of disappointment, including home care, primary care (family doctors), and accountability.[4]

THREATS TO LEAN HEALTHCARE SUCCESS

Frankly, healthcare has viewed quality and capacity in a very naïve manner. The successes noted earlier in this book are all cases of overcoming these threats, whether or not they were explicitly recognized.

Quality has typically been addressed by reducing the number of *presenting* problems (treating the symptoms and not the root causes). And capacity has typically been addressed by asking for more money for more capacity—more beds, more physicians, more nurses, and so forth.

In either case, these views have precluded the search for true root causes that can be permanently fixed with appropriate countermeasures. In effect, healthcare has become used to managing problems and not eliminating them. It is hard to overemphasize the important difference between managing problems and eliminating them. Healthcare has become very good at managing, not eliminating, problems—to its detriment.

For example, consider the revolving bed crises, the hospital infections crises, or the reappearance of problems that were once considered resolved. How many healthcare problems are old problems that had only the symptoms treated? Band-Aids might belong in a home first aid kit, but they are not permanent countermeasures that reduce problems to zero. Does a 2010 model year Toyota still have the problems of a 1970 Toyota? No. Neither should healthcare.

There are two roots causes for the delay of Lean healthcare.

Poor Thinking about Staffing and Quality

The logic has been that people shortages lead to quality issues and wait times. If hospitals had more people, it has been argued, quality would go up and wait times would go down. Hospitals have been facing severe shortages of key skilled employees, including nurses, pharmacists, and medical technologists. Some of this is the result of shifting demographic patterns. Consider retirement rates. It is estimated that that by 2012–2013, half the people working as nurses will have left for retirement. Adding people to address quality will not work. Cutting positions to balance budgets will not work, either.

Poor Thinking about Capacity and Quality

When trying to address wait times, hospitals usually ask for more capacity.

ER waiting, access to radiation therapy, surgical procedures, and other wait times were thought to be best answered by adding capacity—more machines, more beds, and more funding. The typical answers have been to add more diagnostic equipment—x-ray, radiation therapy, MRI, CAT scan equipment or more beds, new buildings, renovations or additions, and more. Adding this type of "capacity" will not work.

Medical Decision-Making Biases

The above root causes are linked to a number of medical decision-making biases.

Using Dysfunctional Decision Making

Kevin Patterson[5] warned about the risks of allowing biases in medical decision making. He noted that:

> The point isn't that some medical treatments don't work as well as it is thought, or even that in treating patients, doctors sometimes hurt them—this has always been true. The point is that the conclusions doctors reach from clinical experience and day-to-day observation of patients are often not reliable. The vast majority of medical therapies, it is now clear, have never been evaluated by systematic study and are used simply because doctors have always believed that they work.

The impact (and truthfulness) of this can be seen in recent reversals about the efficacy of hormone replacement therapy and arthroscopic knee surgery, to name only two items with a large impact.

Rushing to Diagnose

The rush to diagnose, to proceed with the familiar (and fall victim to decision-making biases), means that the healthcare community can be said to work harder and costlier to make poorer decisions.

Promoting Healthcare Professionals to Managerial Roles

Making matters worse is when healthcare professionals are promoted to managerial positions. They bring these same biases to organizational decision making.

Using Healthcare People to Drive Lean

Healthcare leaders and practitioners insist that Lean teams should incorporate seasoned healthcare professionals. This is wrong for three reasons:

1. Healthcare professionals are not good at process improvement or organizational change because they don't come from Lean or behavioral sciences backgrounds.
2. Healthcare professionals often fail to listen to those at the gemba (closest to production) level—the staff and patients who have the real expertise.
3. Healthcare professionals treat organizational *symptoms* and not the *true root causes* that can lead to sustainable countermeasures and improvements.

To be clear, the healthcare profession is truly full of people who care deeply about the health and recovery of their patients. However, measurements of productivity are like accident statistics. They tell you there is a problem, but they don't do anything about the accidents.

Successful healthcare leaders who build Lean into their organizations can realize huge and sustainable benefits. Lean is likely the only method by which their organizations can overcome the global healthcare challenges introduced above.

SUCCESS OF LEAN IN HEALTHCARE

For Lean success to be carried across the globe, healthcare leaders need to drive home the importance of sustainable culture change. Lean is not a fad or a program. It is the culture of continuous improvement—a journey, not a destination.

Hospitals that have been successful at dealing with challenges have implemented Lean and have seen patients and staff benefits. They have lowered costs, kept savings, and responded to growing demand for services in the face of shrinking tax contributions. These hospitals are building on experience and similarities to the manufacturing sector.

A Lean in Healthcare Success Story: Virginia Mason Medical Center

Consider Virginia Mason Medical Center (VMMC) in Seattle, Washington. It has been using Lean management principles for several years (Table 13.1). Using Lean to eliminate waste and make problems visible, VMMC eliminated the need for planned expansions by creating capacity.

In addition, VMMS also saved:

- $1 million by eliminating the need for an additional hyperbaric chamber
- $1 to $3 million for proposed endoscopy suites relocations
- $6 million for new surgery suites whose capacity was found in existing "bricks and mortar"

TABLE 13.1

Results of 175 Rapid Process Improvement Weeks at VMMC

Category	2004 Results—After Two Years of Lean	Metric	Change from 2002
Inventory	1,350,000	Dollars	Down 53%
Productivity	158	FTEs	36% redeployed to other open positions
Floor space	22,324	Sq. Ft.	Down 41%
Lead time	23,082	Hours	Down 65%
People distance	Traveled 267,793	Feet	Down 44%
Product distance	Traveled 272,262	Feet	Down 72%
Setup time	7,744	Hours	Down 82%

Source: http://www.ids-healthcare.com/Common/Paper/Paper_51/Going%20Lean%20in%20Health%20Care1.htm.

LEAN HEALTHCARE FUTURE

Healthcare centers, hospitals, and medical groups must break free from a "business as usual" mentality. Here is my personal prescription for healthcare leaders:

1. Healthcare leaders need to build Lean cultures that promote the search for waste in healthcare. They can help their teams and employees to apply the economic concepts of efficiency and effectiveness to redirect resources. It's as simple as finding Lean savings and eliminating the budget silos that prevent savings from one area being used to address the needs of other areas.

2. They must look hard at their human performance management systems in order to drive home the accountability for process improvement and shed the "That's not my job" mentality. Given the huge levels of waste in working time for nurses, for example, there must be a transition from "sit and wait" to actively addressing continuous improvement. Idle time is waste, plain and simple.

3. They have to encourage their employees to look at other sectors and drive out the biases that have plagued medical decision making and Lean implementation efforts to date. This will lead to fact-based decision making, with people going to the source of the problem (gemba), and using realistic approaches to problem solving so that root causes are revealed and countermeasures can be permanent. This includes a strong effort on moving away from treating symptoms, not root causes. In one case, I was called in as a consultant to fix a critical backlog problem. The previous consultants had ordered overtime to reduce the backlog and claimed that as a Lean success. However, they'd tackled only the symptom, not the root cause. My team fixed the root cause.

4. They should look at internal transformation as a precondition for meaningful Lean health system reform. Do not rely on in-house experts, who are likely to repeat earlier failures. Drive the internal change with select partners who know Lean, can help with organizational change as a result of behavioral science backgrounds, and have demonstrated an ability to help throughout the Lean journey.

5. They must use Lean both to rise above the current challenges and to meet the new imperatives of the medical marketplace, such as medical tourism, multilevel healthcare, mobility in the patient populations, and new competition for healthcare and related services (such as lab work or medical assessments).

The global healthcare sector must look to internal resources to reduce costs and increase net revenues because there simply aren't any other options. Quality of care must increase in the face of diverse challenges. We know that Lean can meet these challenges because we know it *has met those challenges* in healthcare and other sectors. We know the prescription for healthcare, and it's Lean.

REFERENCES

1. NIH, NHLBI Obesity Education Initiative. Clinical guidelines on the identification, evaluation, and treatment of overweight and obesity in adults. http://www.nhlbi.nih.gov/guidelines/obesity/ob_gdlns.pdf.
2. Corrigan, J., L. Kohn, and M. Donaldson, eds. 1999. To err is human: Building a safer health system. Committee on Quality of Health Care in America, Institute of Medicine, Washington, D.C.: National Academies Press.
3. CBC News, Quebec health minister inspired by Toyota philosophy: Management approach used in Boston, Pittsburgh, Seattle hospitals. http://www.cbc.ca/canada/montreal/story/2008/07/10/qc-healthminister0910.html.
4. *Globe and Mail.* 2008. Health care's appetite, Friday, November 13.
5. Patterson, K. 2002. What doctors don't know (almost everything). *New York Times*, Health. May 5.

Glossary

5S: Sort, Set in order, Shine, Standardize, and Sustain. These activities are used by organizations to achieve and maintain continuous improvement. The focus of these activities is to organize the work area in order to make it more efficient.

A3 problem solving: A structured process improvement method. A team records the results of investigation and planning in a concise, two-page document—the A3 report—that facilitates knowledge sharing and collaboration.

A3 report: See A3 problem solving.

Actual lead time: The overall time it takes to provide a service.

Affinity chart: See Affinity diagram.

Affinity diagram: A graphic tool designed to help organize loose, unstructured ideas generated in brainstorming or problem-solving meetings. In this method, disparate but related ideas (collected in an idea generation session) are grouped (on cards or sheets of paper) into meaningful categories called affinity sets. These categories tie different concepts together with one underlying theme, clarify the issues, and provide a structure for a systematic search for one or more solutions. Also called an affinity chart.

Brainstorming: A problem-solving technique where a group works together to develop ideas on a specific problem. Brainstorming can take two forms—structured or unstructured. In a structured brainstorming session, each person in the team is asked to generate ideas and solutions. Unstructured brainstorming allows any member of the group to contribute at any time.

CAP: See Change and acceleration process (CAP).

Cause-and-effect diagram: A problem-solving technique that enables you to depict all the possible causes of a specific problem graphically. The causes are depicted as "fish bones." Each of the "bones" or causes corresponds to the 4Ms—Manpower, Machine, Materials, and Methods. This tool should be used when the primary symptom of a problem is known, but possible causes are unclear.

Change acceleration process (CAP): A Six Sigma tool that can be used in the implementation of the DMAIC system. It is used to help ensure that the entire organization will accept and be comfortable with the improvement initiative and the changes that it is proposing. All stakeholders are analyzed to try and identify any issues or concerns that they may have with the new improvement strategies. You can then develop a strategy to address these potential barriers so that the targeted processes and areas can be changed effectively.

Changeover time: The time taken in each operation or step to readjust and reset equipment before the next set of material/patient/information arrives for processing or consultation.

Cheat sheet: See Tip sheet.

Crib sheet: See Tip sheet.

Current state map: Used in value stream mapping. A graphic illustration of an organization's current process.

Cycle time: The time spent actually working (adding value) on the product or service.

Dashboard: A web-based technology page on which real-time information is collated from various sources in the business. The metaphor of dashboard emphasizes the nature of the data being displayed on the page. It is a real-time analysis of how a business is operating, just like an automobile dashboard displays real-time information about the vehicle's performance.

Define Measure Analyze Improve Control (DMAIC): One of the main quality systems used in Six Sigma. It provides a methodology for achieving continuous improvement.

Deming cycle: See Plan Do Check Act (PDCA).

Deming wheel: See Plan Do Check Act (PDCA).

Design for Six Sigma (DFSS): A model that focuses on designing new processes with Six Sigma quality levels.

DFSS: See Design for Six Sigma (DFSS).

Discrete event simulation: A simulation of events, in which the highest-priority event is removed from an event queue and executed. This may have the effect of scheduling future events.

DMAIC: See Define Measure Analyze Improve Control (DMAIC).

Electronic Patient Record (EPR): A healthcare record stored in electronic format.

EPR: See Electronic patient record (EPR).

External setup/changeover activities: Elements in a setup or change-over that can be performed only when equipment or resources are occupied.

Failure mode and effect analysis (FMEA): A Six Sigma procedure that is used to identify every possible failure mode of a process. It aims to determine the effect on other subitems and on the required function of the product, service, or process. It is also used to rank the causes of failures and develop and implement preventive actions.

FIFO: See First-in/first-out (FIFO).

First-in-first-out (FIFO): A philosophy based on the principle that the first piece of inventory, supply, unit of work, or patient required in a process is delivered first.

Fish bone diagram: See Cause-and-effect diagram.

Flowchart: A common type of chart that represents an algorithm or process, showing the steps as boxes of various kinds, and their order by connecting these with arrows. Flowcharts are used in analyzing, designing, documenting, or managing a process or program in various fields.

FMEA: See Failure mode and effect analysis (FMEA).

Future state map: Used in value stream mapping. A graphic illustration of an organization's desired performance.

Gallup survey: A public opinion poll. Although originated by Dr. George Gallup, the term has taken on a more generic meaning.

Graham flowchart: A flowchart produced using Graham Process Mapping Software. This is software that enables the user to produce detailed process maps for documenting, developing, improving, and managing business processes.

Ideal state map: Used in value stream mapping. A graphic illustration of how the process would look if perfect integration of all components were to occur.

Internal setup activities: Elements in the changeover or setup that can be carried out only when the equipment or resource is stopped or in a state where it cannot be used for another task.

Inventory: The actual product, service, supply, or raw material located at different stages in a process.

JIT: See Just-in-time (JIT).

Just-in-time (JIT): An inventory strategy implemented to improve the return on investment of a business by reducing in-process inventory and its associated carrying costs. To achieve JIT, the process must have signals of what is going on elsewhere within the process.

Kaizen: The philosophy focused on problem solving to achieve gradual, orderly, and continuous improvement throughout all the elements of a process.

Kaizen event: A carefully planned, well-structured team-based activity focused on solving problems by identifying any elements of waste in a process and eliminating these elements in as short a period of time as possible.

Kanban: A system where production is authorized from downstream operations, based on physical consumption. It is based on a pull material replenishment system, with the principle that supplies or resources are pulled through the process based on the actual client or patient requirements.

Lean: The removal of waste or non-value-added activities in a process.

Lean Thinking: The systematic approach to identifying and eliminating waste or non-value-added activities through continuous improvement. This is achieved by enabling the flow of a product or service at the pull of the client in pursuit of perfection.

Leveling: The process required to average both the volume and sequence of different operations, steps, resources, or work loads in a process.

Lightning strike: Comments that are added to the future state map outlining improvement ideas or initiatives for a process.

Non-value-added activity: Any activity that does not add value to a product or service from the client's or patient's perspective.

Ohno circle: A process developed by Taiichi Ohno, the Toyota executive largely responsible for structuring and implementing the system known today as the Toyota Production System over four decades after World War II. Ohno was known for drawing a chalk circle around managers and making them stand in the circle until they had seen and documented all the problems in a particular area.

Operational research (OR): An interdisciplinary branch of applied mathematics and formal science that uses methods such as mathematical modeling, statistics, and algorithms to arrive at optimal or near optimal solutions to complex problems. It is typically concerned with optimizing the maxima (profit, assembly line performance, crop yield, bandwidth, etc.) or minima (loss, risk, etc.) of some objective function. It helps management achieve its goals using scientific methods.

Opportunity time: The potential non-process time that can be eliminated from a value stream process.

OR: See Operational research (OR).

Par level: The "average" or "normal" amount. When considering maintaining a certain level of stock, the par level is the amount you would need to have on hand to ensure that you would not run out while waiting for new supplies. The par level is also the order point.

Pareto analysis: A problem-solving technique based on a data-driven approach to focus resources on the area that offers the greatest potential for improvement. It is based on the proven Pareto principle that 20 percent of the sources cause 80 percent of the problem. It also provides a way of displaying the relative importance of each problem in a visual format.

Pareto chart: A special type of bar chart where the values being plotted are arranged in descending order. The graph is accompanied by a line graph that shows the cumulative totals of each category, left to right. The chart is named after Vilfredo Pareto, and its use in quality assurance was popularized by Joseph M. Juran and Kaoru Ishikawa.

PDCA: See Plan Do Check Act (PDCA).

Perfection: An ongoing activity to achieve better results.

Plan Do Check Act (PDCA): An iterative four-step problem-solving process typically used in business process improvement. It is also known as the Deming cycle, Shewhart cycle, or Deming wheel.

Poka Yoke: A system that uses simple, low-cost devices to reduce errors. It is used to prevent defective parts from being made or passed into the process.

Product or service family: A group of products or services that pass through similar processing steps and over common equipment and resources in an organization's downstream process.

Pull: A system of a cascading process or supply chain from downstream to upstream activities in which nothing is produced by the upstream supplier until the downstream client signals a need.

Quality at source: A technique that reduces the need for rework and prevents further work and cost on a product that is already defective.

Resource leveling: A process focused on the most effective use of resources in process to ensue optimum flow.

Run chart: A graph that displays observed data in a time sequence. Often, the data displayed represents some aspect of the output or performance of a manufacturing or other business process. Also known as a run-sequence plot.

Run-sequence plot: See Run chart.

Set in order: The second stage in a 5S program. The aim of this stage is to organize the workplace to ensure that there is a place for everything.

Shewhart cycle: See Plan Do Check Act (PDCA).

Shine: The third stage in a 5S program. The aim of this stage is to clean, inspect, and maintain everything in the work area on a regular basis to ensure quality and safety.

Sigma: A measurement of standard deviation.

Single minute exchange of dies (SMED): A practice aimed at reducing the time lost during setups and changeovers.

Six Sigma: A quality system often used in conjunction with Lean Thinking. It is a powerful suite of process interrogation and performance management tools and systems aimed at reducing product and service variation.

SMED: See Single minute exchange of dies (SMED).

Sort: The first stage in a 5S program. The aim of this stage is to eliminate any unnecessary materials from the workplace.

Spaghetti diagram: A problem-solving tool used to trace and depict the paths and flow of information, supplies, and resources (equipment and people) throughout a process with the aim of identifying opportunities to optimize flow.

Stakeholder: An individual or group with an interest in maintaining the success of an organization and upholding the viability of the organization's products and services.

Standardize: The fourth stage in a 5S program. The aim of this stage is to make all work areas consistent with each other through the development of standards, guidelines, and practices for implementing and maintaining 5S.

Standardized work: The documentation and application of best practices for a process.

Storyboard: A graphic organizer, such as a series of illustrations or images displayed in sequence, which is used to visualize a sequence.

Sustain: The final stage in a 5S program. This stage is ongoing and is aimed at maintaining continued compliance with 5S standards and practices that have been developed.

Takt time: The average rate at which clients buy products or consume services. It is also the rate at which products should be manufactured or services delivered.

TAT: See Turnaround time (TAT).

Tip sheet: A concise set of notes used for quick reference. Also known as a cheat sheet or crib sheet.

Total productive maintenance (TPM): The philosophy and practice of preventing the loss of productive machine time.

TPM: See Total productive maintenance (TPM).

Turnaround time (TAT): The time between the placement of an order and its delivery.

Value: An element in a process that the client or patient is willing to pay for.

Value stream: The end-to-end collection of processes that creates value for the client or patient.

Value stream design (VSD): A method used to visualize the whole picture and improve it—within the organization and beyond. VSD helps the user to develop and implement new competitive and customer-oriented value streams.

Value stream investigation (VSI): An event that occurs at the start of a Lean implementation. It enables those involved to establish the current state of the organization's processes and enables the organization to assess whether any areas need more detailed investigation.

Value stream mapping (VSM): A primary Lean tool that describes the flow of material and information through a system. This is carried out by graphically portraying the current process, enabling one to see where value is added and lost.

Value stream plan: A strategy and schedule for realizing the future state of a process.

Value-added activity: Any activity that is aimed at creating value for the client or patient.

Visual management: A system that enables anyone to immediately assess the current status of an operation or process at a glance, regardless of the person's knowledge of that process.

VOC: See Voice of the customer (VOC).

Voice of the customer (VOC): A Six Sigma tool that can be used in the define stage of the DMAIC system. The technique gathers input from customers and patients affected by a process to establish their needs and requirements and to define aims and goals for process improvements based on these.

VSD: See Value stream design (VSD).

VSI: See Value stream investigation (VSI).

VSM: See Value stream mapping (VSM).

Waste: Any element of a process that adds time, effort, or cost but no value.

Work balancing: The process required to utilize the workload associated with resources in a process—staff, equipment, supplies, and so forth—to meet patient requirements most effectively.

Y2K: The Year 2000 problem (also known as the Y2K problem, the millennium bug, or the Y2K bug) was a notable computer bug resulting from the practice in early computer program design of representing the year with two digits. This caused some date-related processing to operate incorrectly for dates and times on and after January 1, 2000 and on other critical dates, which were billed "event horizons."

Editors

Joe Aherne is a fellow and council member of the Institute of Certified Public Accountants in Ireland. He established The Leading Edge Group in 1995 as a niche boutique consulting and education company supporting the multinational and healthcare sectors. The group is now recognized as one of the largest Lean accreditation organizations of its kind, successfully supporting the education of students of all nationalities in the areas of Lean Manufacturing and Lean Healthcare. Joe is a regular speaker at international conferences and seminars and is an avid believer in the power of Lean Healthcare.

John Whelton has a postgraduate diploma in technical communications, and has more than ten years' experience in instructional design and the development of distance, online, and blended learning solutions. He is currently spearheading the expansion of The Leading Edge Group operations in North America and is located in Toronto, Canada. He has previously held key roles in product development with leading learning solutions providers CBT Systems, SmartForce, and SkillSoft. John was recently involved in coordinating the development of our Lean Healthcare Green Belt and Black Belt programs.

The Leading Edge Group Lean Healthcare Programs: How can you support the future sustainability of Lean in your organization? What kind of learning can you engage in to further enhance your career development? The Leading Edge Group, in association with professional institutes and academic institutions, offers the following programs for those involved in continuous improvement initiatives within healthcare.

- Lean Healthcare Yellow Belt Program
- Lean Healthcare Green Belt Program
- Lean Healthcare Black Belt Program
- Customized Lean Healthcare Workshops
- Lean Healthcare Transformation Programs

For more information, please e-mail info@leanhealthcareservices.com or contact our customer service teams at the following numbers: Europe: +353 21 4855863; North America: +1 416 637 5074.

Contributors

Christian Buchsteiner is a healthcare improvement coordinator at PeaceHealth, in Eugene, Oregon. Born in Salzburg, Austria, he completed his BSc in mechanical engineering. He started his professional career with Sony DADC Austria, where he spent seventeen years managing different manufacturing processes. In June 2002, Christian moved from Austria to Eugene, Oregon, and accepted a role with Oregon Medical Laboratories (OML), to oversee and streamline the preanalytical laboratory process and to support the laboratory move to its new location in 2006. In 2007, he took up the post of healthcare improvement coordinator with PeaceHealth in Oregon. In this role he designs the patient-centered and Lean processes required for the PeaceHealth move to its new state-of-the-art hospital.

John Coleman, MSc, MBA, FRSA, and **Tim Franklin, MBA, FRSA,** come from a strong technical background of science and engineering, and they have created a unique set of change management skills and abilities. This combines both the "hard" science and "soft" behavioral issues of change. These skills were developed and honed in various senior management and board-level roles in both public and international private sector organizations. Tim and John have been working together for a number of years, successfully deploying their joint skills with clients in a variety of sectors. In January 2007, they formed Alturos Ltd. With a growing team of seventeen skilled and experienced associates or employees, Alturos has successfully helped many organizations to create organizational development and continuous improvement programs. Alturos has been particularly active within the U.K. National Health Service, where it is working with acute trusts, PCTs, mental health trusts, and shared services providers.

Simon Dodds is a consultant surgeon at Heart of England National Health Service (NHS) Foundation Trust in the United Kingdom. He is a 1982 graduate of Cambridge University with a degree in medicine and computer science. He qualified as a doctor at St. Bartholomew's Hospital in London. He was appointed a consultant vascular surgeon at Good Hope

Hospital in 1999, and five years later, he and his team were awarded the first NHS Innovation Award for Service Improvement, for the redesign of the vascular outpatient clinic and development and implementation of the North Birmingham leg ulcer telemedicine service. In 2006, Simon published a short book called *Three Wins*, which retold the story of his journey, and it was during the background reading for the book that he came across the terms "Lean Thinking," "Theory of Constraints," and "Six Sigma." In late 2006, Good Hope Hospital agreed to support an evaluation of Lean training and application of the rapid improvement framework to elderly patients who had accidentally broken their hips. In 2007, Good Hope Hospital merged with the neighboring Heart of England NHS Foundation Trust and has since created its own Lean Academy to help catalyze the transformation process. See Chapter 11 for another case study involving Good Hope Hospital.

Franciscan Health System (FHS) consisted of three hospitals in the south Puget Sound area. The hospitals were St. Francis Hospital (110 beds), St. Joseph Medical Center (320 beds), and St. Clare Hospital (106 beds). Collectively, this system made up twenty-two units (including emergency department and pharmacy).

Hilary Grey is director of clinical operations for Aptium Cancer Care, Cheshire, England. She graduated in 1983 with a BSc in nursing from the University of Witwatersrand in South Africa. Hilary began her career as a district nurse and then specialized in the area of care for patients with cancer. In 1991, she moved to the United States and began a career with Aptium Oncology (formerly known as Salick Health Care). At Aptium, Hilary gained a vast amount of operational experience, finally moving into the role of vice president of clinical services at the Aptium corporate office. She undertook an MBA program at the University of Maryland to help bridge what she perceived as knowledge gaps. In 2005, she moved to the United Kingdom as part of a team designated to set up a subsidiary of Aptium.

Timothy D. Hill, PhD, is a recognized leader in Lean best practices and human capital. His work as an international consulting industrial and organizational psychologist has literally spanned the globe. His push to connect best practices from Lean and human capital was motivated by the need to connect people and processes. Beginning in the 1980s, Tim spent large portions of his time in the Far East. He has worked with Toyota for more than twenty years in Canada, China, Japan, and the United States. While working in North America and the Far East, he partnered with Toyota, Matsushita, Motorola, and others to study quality and production practices. He also studied at the Asian Productivity Organization, the W. Edwards Deming Institute, the Kaizen Institute, the Japanese Association of Suggestion Systems, the Quality Control Research Institute, Japan, and the Japanese Union of Scientists and Engineers (JUSE) in order to bring Kaizen, Lean manufacturing, quality control, Six Sigma, TBP, TPM, TPS, TQM, TQC, and more to production, professional, and service settings. Tim worked with Dr. Deming, Ishikawa, Imai, and other world-quality leaders. His influential research paper (Hill, T. D. 1988. Is it finally time to recognize F.W. Taylor? Department of Psychology Research Bulletin 668, University of Western Ontario, London, Ontario, Canada) built on work in the early 1980s and showed a "Lean" connection that dated back to the late 1800s.

Mimi Kokoska, MD, is the Veterans Integrated System Network 11 surgical consultant and chief of otolaryngology head and neck surgery at the Richard L. Roudebush VA Medical Center, Indianapolis, Indiana. She is also professor in the Department of Otolaryngology Head and Neck Surgery, Indiana University School of Medicine. She received her Green Belt in Lean Healthcare in 2008 and she continues to promote, implement, and teach Lean Thinking in an academic and veterans' hospital setting.

Deborah Miller is the owner of a professional services consulting firm that works with leaders to organize their business processes, set goals, use resources wisely, and achieve results that matter. She offers services tailored to the unique needs of an organization, using her expertise in process and quality improvement, project management, and communication. Deborah received a master's degree from Purdue University and her Six Sigma Black Belt from Sigma Breakthrough Technologies, Inc. She recently completed an International Green Belt in Lean Healthcare certification with The Leading Edge Group.

Brendan Murphy is a national organization development and design manager within the human resource directorate in the Health Service Executive (HSE) in Ireland. Originally a work study officer, Brendan began his career in the clothing and textile industry in Northern Ireland, ultimately managing the work-study function in three factories within the group. In 2006, he completed an MSc in records management at the University of Northumbria and has been actively promoting the importance of this function to his organization, establishing in recent times a group to develop a new national records management strategy. In 2008, he completed a Green Belt in Lean Healthcare certification with The Leading Edge Group to complement his industrial engineering and O&M experience and to provide him with the essential skills for promoting the important concept of Lean in Healthcare.

Carlos F. Pinto is currently the head of the Instituto de Oncologia do Vale (IOV), a medical group focused on oncology ambulatory care with units located in São Jose dos Campos, Taubate, and three other towns in Vale do Paraiba, a region with two million inhabitants in São Paulo State, northeast of São Paulo city. The IOV is one of the first Brazilian fully accredited cancer centers. Carlos has served in many professional and administrative positions: counselor for oncology at São Paulo Medical Council (1995–98); president of the Brazilian Clinical Oncology Society (SBOC), São Paulo Branch (1997–99); planning secretariat for the SBOC (1999–2001); and treasurer for the SBOC (2001–2003). He is still serving at the HRVP high council and quality branch.

Teresa Stevens, BA, is a management and program analyst at the Department of Veterans Affairs. She graduated from Mississippi State University in 1989 with a degree in accounting. She received her Green Belt in Lean Healthcare after completing a project that improved patient flow through the emergency department at the Central Arkansas Veterans Healthcare System.

Samuel B. Welch, MD, PhD, is an assistant chief of surgery at Central Arkansas Veteran's Healthcare System (CAVHS) in Little Rock, Arkansas. He is also an associate professor and residency program director of Otolaryngology (Head and Neck Surgery) at the University of Arkansas for Medical Sciences (UAMS) in Little Rock. His interest in Lean Thinking was sparked by his personal desire to "make a positive difference" in the healthcare of veterans and the education of medical students and residents.

Kelley Williamson holds a BFA degree from the University of Kansas and is a human resources manager, Inpatient Business Partner for the University of Colorado Hospital. She holds a Green Belt in Lean Healthcare and a Green Belt in Lean Six Sigma. She has more than twenty years of successful leadership and management experience, including performance management, sales, process improvement, and organizational development with such companies as Software Spectrum, Expanets, Business Technology Consultants, and RELERA. Kelley's broad range of experience at the University of Colorado Hospital includes leadership and management competencies, customer service, Lean initiatives, human performance improvement initiatives, and the development of a performance excellence process for leadership. Kelley leads the following programs: patient satisfaction scores initiative; all university grant learning (totaling $8 million); culture and transition teams; capacity management and throughput, rate and ranking for inpatients.

Judy-Ann Wybenga is the senior regional manager of site operations for the nutrition and food services department in the David Thompson health region (DTHR). She is a 1981 graduate of the School of Hotel and Food Administration at the University of Guelph in Ontario, with a Bachelor of Commerce, majoring in institutional food service management. Her administrative dietetic internship was completed at the Misericordia Hospital in Edmonton, Alberta in 1982. Judy-Ann completed her Masters of Business Administration at the University of Alberta in 1991. In the spring of 2007 she was invited to participate on a seven-member Lean team to study work processes in lab services. The experience of "learning to see" based on Lean principles fundamentally changed her management style. Obtaining her Green Belt in Lean Healthcare in April 2008 from The Leading Edge Group was an excellent opportunity to validate her field experience. She focused on how to apply Lean Thinking to the food service operations.

Index